E. J. KAHN, JR.

KAHN, Ely Jacques, Jr. **The first decade; a report on independent black Africa.** Norton, 1972. 192p map 79-38542. 7.95. ISBN 0-393-05468-3

CHOICE   DEC. '72

History, Geography & Travel

 Africa

A fast-moving journalistic account written by a staff writer of the *New Yorker* magazine, containing much well-informed and accurate information. The book moves rapidly among topics, countries, and vignettes of one kind or another. Yet, one is given a realistic sense of the dynamics, problems, and flavor of the contemporary African continent. The book is very readable, a lively and surprisingly intelligently informed journalist's quick-eyed view of the many complexities and contradictions found in East and West Africa today. Highly recommended for leisure-time reading both for the student of African affairs as well as the novice interested in the world around him.

THE
FIRST
DECADE

A REPORT ON
INDEPENDENT BLACK AFRICA

E. J. KAHN, JR.

W · W · NORTON & COMPANY · INC ·
NEW YORK

Copyright © 1972 by E. J. Kahn, Jr.

FIRST EDITION

Library of Congress Cataloging in Publication Data
Kahn, Ely Jacques, 1916–
  The first decade.
  1. Africa, Sub-Saharan—Politics. 2. Africa,
Sub-Saharan—Economic conditions—1918-
I. Title.
DT352.8.K34   320.9'67   79-38542
ISBN 0-393-05468-3

Published simultaneously in Canada
by George J. McLeod Limited, Toronto

Much of the material in this book appeared, in somewhat different form, in *The New Yorker*.

PRINTED IN THE UNITED STATES OF AMERICA

1 2 3 4 5 6 7 8 9 0

FOR ELLIE

AUTHOR'S
NOTE

If Africa is in some respects the most backward of continents, it is in others the most forward-looking. Perhaps never before has an area so complex and heterogeneous tried to move so far so fast. Africa is big, and some of its thinkers think big. In Nairobi, I spent a couple of entertaining and enlightening hours with one of the continent's more worldly and imaginative young writers, Taban Lo Liyong, a Ugandan now living in Kenya. He studied for a while in the United States, mostly at Iowa State University, where he worked in a library by day and wrote by night. There was a nine-cup coffee pot in his room, and he sometimes went through three pots at a stretch.

Once, he told me, while he was composing a long poem, he stayed awake for forty hours. Then he dozed off at his job, on his feet with his arms upraised, holding a stack of books he was supposed to shelve. It must have been quite a feat, but his supervisor was unimpressed and, after delivering a tart lecture on the American virtues of hustle and bustle, asked why he was so sleepy. Lo Liyong said he'd been writing a poem. The librarian asked to see it, read it, and fired him for all-around incompetence. It is hard these days to be an African in a world dominated by Western values.

9

Lo Liyong spent more than five years in America. "Most of my best friends were in the library," he told me. He did not mean librarians; he meant books. All in all, his literary relationships seemed to have been happier than his human ones. At the time of our meeting, he had not long before been divorced from a woman for whom, since she had a British education, he had been obliged to pay a whacking bride price: five thousand shillings and fifty cows. Born in 1939, Lo Liyong regarded himself as a "young elder" —a man who could at once articulate the feelings of African youth and analyze the problems of adult African society. In his view, young Africans were, commendably, becoming increasingly rational and decreasingly influenced by ancient tribal mythologies—were, that was, becoming more and more de-Africanized. He pointed out with satisfaction that the English department at the University of Nairobi, where he lectured, was offering courses in Oriental, Caribbean, and American literature, not to mention Japanese poetry— this last in part to keep the intellectual community in tune with the mounting African demand for Honda motorcycles.

Lo Liyong thought that Africans had to stop dealing in clichés and start dealing in rationalities. "Africa has its past," he said, "and that's important, but it also has its future, and that's more important. The future can only be constructed through the present, and the present demands a rational outlook. We have no Shakespeare yet among our writers, for instance, but it would be foolish for us to sit around and wait for one to come along. We're writing what we write so that when an authentic genius materializes he'll have our shoulders to stand on."

Lo Liyong had recently published a collection of essays, *The Last Word*, which had gone into a second printing and was, by African standards, a best-seller. For the first five months after publication, though, his royalties from it had amounted to just twenty-five hundred shillings—about three hundred and fifty dollars. In the book, he reflected comparatively and provocatively on the futures of the African and American continents: "And when we reach the Twenty-first Century we shall arrive there without our kings and aristocrats (isn't that why Nkrumah demoted feudal lords?), we shall arrive there without serfs (isn't that why Uganda kings had to go?), we shall arrive there without tribes (isn't that the test going on in Nigeria, Kenya, Sudan, now?). By the time the Twenty-first Century comes—that century of the man of equal privileges—Africa might offer more to each individual citizen while the white Appalachian poor might still roam the hillsides, migrant farmers might still be underpaid, ghetto Negroes might still room with rats."

Trying to form an impression of my own of what black Africa was like roughly a decade after independence, and to have a look at the evolving middle of the continent before it shot or skidded or sank into the Twenty-first Century, in which it seems bound one way or another to play a consequential role, I spent nine and a half weeks there at the end of 1970 and the beginning of 1971. I started at its western terminus, Dakar, and moved across it, stopping off at fourteen countries, to the Indian Ocean at Mombasa and Dar es Salaam, thence southwest to Lusaka, and finally back up northeast to Addis Ababa. My wife, the writer Eleanor Munro, accompanied me, and as all wives should, she contributed periodically to the maintenance of my humility. At the American Embassy in Monrovia one day, for instance, I left her for a few minutes in the office of the Deputy Chief of Mission. Returning to fetch her, I had got as far as the D. C. M.'s outer office when I overheard him telling someone on the phone that there was a distinguished American author on the premises. I paused to hear more, and as he went on flatteringly I beamed at his secretary and pointed to myself in mock self-deprecation. A moment later, the D. C. M. spoke the name of the person he'd been complimenting —my wife.

I did not recover my self-confidence until I was on the road one day between Kaduna, in northern Nigeria, and Lagos, the Nigerian capital. Nigeria is a tricky country to drive in—one academy for tyro motorists is aptly called the Uphill Driving School—so I had engaged a car and an indigenous driver for the five-hundred-and-fifty-mile journey, which took eighteen hours. I was put in my place at the outset when the driver, on learning that I merely wanted to be delivered to Lagos, informed me loftily that the last "master" who had hired him—it was his word, not mine—had paused en route to shoot a crocodile. I felt that something special was demanded

11

of me. My chance came when we broke down fifty miles north of Ibadan. The highway's savage potholes had jarred loose some vital part of the engine, and my man said we'd be stuck for sure unless he could re-secure it with a piece of wire, but where in this desolate tract could one hope to find anything like that? I saved the day by removing my suitcase from the trunk, digging out a wire coat-hanger, and presenting it to him with a lordly flourish. For the rest of the trip, he accorded me the heady reverence one would normally expect for outwrestling a leopard.

It is difficult for a Westerner, unless he has a great deal of time and energy, to come to grips with the greater part of Africa—that Africa of the bush, of subsistence agriculture, the Africa largely invisible from the roads and all but incomprehensible from the airports. But as I say, I had only a relatively short time to roam and look and listen. I'd have felt guiltier than I do about the brevity of my stay had I not, in Nairobi, had lunch with a United States Congressman who was spending twenty-four hours in Kenya while on a fact-finding tour of the continent. And how many more days was he devoting to the rest of Africa, I asked. Two, he said. Another lunch, in Zambia, also made me feel much better. This one was with an Englishman who had lived in Africa for thirty years. On ascertaining that I was a writer, he asked me if I had a book in mind about my trip. It was too soon to say for certain, I replied, but in any event I felt embarrassed even to be discussing the possibility in his learned company. "Don't be silly," he said. "The longer one stays in Africa, the less one knows about it." The pages that follow, then, can in a sense be attributed to his kind encouragement.

—E. J. K.

Truro, Mass.
10 November 1971

THE
FIRST
DECADE

1

It is tempting, but dangerous, to generalize about continents, perhaps more so about Africa than any other. A half dozen black men walking along a street in Lagos, Kinshasa, or Nairobi may seem at a glance to be very much the same, but the differences among them may actually be as profound as those among any six individuals on earth. They may have utterly dissimilar concepts of social units or of the ownership of land—two matters of possibly more concern to all of them than the Suez Canal or Namibia. They may indeed be unable to communicate with one another. Yet they are all black and all African.

The hazards of generalization were impressed sharply on me one day in Tanzania, a briskly emerging nation where, because of its unabashedly socialistic orientation, the American visitor is apt to be especially sensitive to the manner of his reception. There has long been a Chinese Communist presence in Tanzania, viewed by most Tanzanians with equanimity, and also an American presence, viewed sometimes with misgiving. (One of our Embassy people was overheard telling another that he had the ammunition ready for a certain occasion. What he meant was that some background papers for a staff conference were prepared, but the words were

taken literally and both men were declared *persona non grata*.)
While I was in Tanzania, staying at the Hotel Kilimanjaro, Dar es
Salaam's finest, I had an appointment at a downtown office building unfamiliar to me. I did have the names of two streets that
intersected at its location. Eluding the African boys who peddle
Chairman Mao's thoughts outside the hotel and sometimes in its
lobby (they approach one with a furtive "Psst," as if they were
selling dirty postcards, and they ask seven shillings—a dollar—for
a small hard-cover edition, though they will take five), I hailed a
cab and specified the intersection I was seeking. The driver nodded
and dropped me off at a corner only two blocks away from the
hotel. It was the wrong intersection, I quickly discovered. Silently
cursing all Africans for their stupidity, I walked into the nearest
store and asked a black clerk for directions. Learning that I was
still a mile from my destination, I muttered something about being
already late, and now without transportation. He hopped up, drove
me to the right place in his own car, and declined a proffered tip.
I silently blessed all Africans for their graciousness. Two generaliza-
tions within minutes, and both of them, on reflection, probably
wrong.

For centuries, the white and yellow peoples of the earth have
satisfied themselves that they have a reasonable capacity for self-
government. It is only in the last decade that more than a relative
handful of blacks have had a chance to show what they can do in
that respect. When I had first been in Africa, in the fall of 1966,
I had been told by white officials of the Republic of South Africa
that they were obliged to administer their country the way they
did because black Africans were really quite incapable of running
things themselves. And after my return home, observing South
Africa from afar, I had noticed how often and with what relish the
runners of things there would dwell upon the coups and counter-
coups and civil wars that would recurrently roil the fledgling black
nations north of the Zambesi River. So it was with special interest
that I set forth to have a look at that enormous and exciting part
of the continent.

A Kenyan not long ago had a letter published in the *East
African Standard*, a Nairobi daily, that went: "The fruit of independence is ripe but very high up on a big tree, and very few

people can reach it. What the poor, hungry, thirsty, and weak African can get out of it is nothing more than its cool shade. I am convinced that our government is strong enough to shake the tree, so that those who are unable to climb it can pick up their share and remember those days when outsiders were their masters." Across the continent, the winds of change have been ruffling the independence tree, and some outsiders consider it remarkable how much fruit that tree has already yielded up. For Kenya and several countries far less advanced have managed in a comparatively few years' span, starting from near rock bottom, to attain a plateau of some security and some stability and considerable legitimacy. To have accomplished that—to have found any answer at all, indeed, to the perplexing problem of how to govern multiracial societies (for whites still figure importantly in African affairs, though now they are usually careful to keep their place)—is little short of phenomenal. As one old African hand, a white Englishman, told me, "You seldom hear these new countries given much credit for what they do, though God knows their mistakes are loudly enough trumpeted, but they've done astonishingly well, having to cope not only with their own tangled internal affairs but with the often competing and selfish activities of great foreign powers with subtle and sophisticated and time-tested approaches; and, above all, in coping with a pervasive and debilitating poverty of a sort incomprehensible to western minds. Such problems have daunted and defeated far larger nations with far greater resources."

A generalization, then, subject to the usual qualifications: Black Africans can run things. They are running things even though their rate of progress was likened by one of them to the ascent of a slippery ladder: "We take two steps up and then one down." They are running things despite the oft-expressed skepticism of biased foreigners: When the phones don't work in the western world, it is an accident; when they don't work in Africa, it is endemic incompetence. (As of course it may sometimes be; I recall trying to make a call from my hotel room in Lomé, Togo, and having the whole instrument come apart in my hand.) They are running them, what is more, despite some massive psychological blocks that afflict many Africans. It was surely one of the most glaring negative aspects of colonialism (there were positive aspects, too) that Africans had little chance to make decisions; even many of those Europeans on the scene who hoped that independence would come to pass suspected that few Africans *could* make a decision, or at any rate a sensible one; and in time many Africans came to entertain those doubts about themselves. After independence, they had scarcely any choice in the matter. They could no longer enjoy the luxury of irresponsibility and irresolution.

By now, many Africans, especially the older ones (over thirty), believe that they can manage quite nicely on their own and, indeed, that the less help they have the better off they'll ultimately be. In Nigeria—a pivotal country in any appraisal of the continent, inasmuch as one out of every five black Africans is a Nigerian—a government official told me, "Unless we decide to be very lazy, we should be able to get along by ourselves fairly soon." Nigeria, to be sure, is a large have nation surrounded by small have-not neighbors, a nation splendidly endowed with oil reserves and all the international clout that that implies; but even so, to have any government man speak unblinkingly of self-sufficiency is startling nowadays. And to hear a black African espouse it north of Pretoria! It was no less startling to hear a reflective white resident of the continent—also, it almost goes without saying, north of Pretoria— say, "You know, if the situation had been reversed and whites had emerged from black colonialism, they probably wouldn't be behaving nearly as well as the blacks are behaving now."

To attain, if not complete self-sufficiency, at least control of their own economies as well as of their governmental processes, Africans are increasingly preaching, and practicing, something called Africanization—or, depending on where the process is in progress, Zambianization or Liberianization or Cameroonization. The replacement of white expatriates at all levels by Africans—in theory, at least, by qualified Africans—has been one of the emerging nations' major goals, and has given them some of their major headaches. When Tanzania, now ardently committed to Tanzanianization, came into being, it had enough African ministers and more than enough African messengers to staff its government departments, but these ends of the bureaucratic sandwich were separated by a thick slab of middle-echelon Europeans. Tanzania is as nationalistic-minded as any of its peers, but like many a young

African country it has concluded that pragmatism abets modernism. Thus, it has encouraged quite a few expatriates to stay around, and has recruited still others. While in the last decade the number of Tanzanian lawyers has increased from three to eighty, they welcome help. The country's Assistant Attorney General is a white Englishman. (He used to be Attorney General, but graciously accepted demotion in the interests of Tanzanianization.) One of that socialistic country's most respected members of Parliament is a white English peeress.

Many an African nation now has a special government agency to expedite the pace of Africanization—e.g., the Executive Zambianization Bureau and the Kenyanization of Personnel Bureau. The understandable impulse to Africanize just about every job Africanizable has led to some odd consequences. Not long ago, the small Jewish community in Nairobi wanted to import a rabbi. The applicants were duly granted the work permit required for non-Africans in Kenya, but they were also informed that they had just a year to Africanize the job. Many of the government ministers across the continent who are most energetically advocating Africanization have balked, however, at giving up their own white European secretaries. Chauvinism is one thing, convenience another. Among some of the ex-colonialists who have been Africanized out of their jobs but have nonetheless stayed around one finds surprisingly little rancor. (The disaffected have presumably defected.) An Englishman residing in Ghana, once a District Commissioner but now merely an advisor, told me cheerfully that he didn't at all mind his change of status. "I enjoyed being a master," he said, "and I enjoy being a servant." The switch in roles, curiously, has seemed harder for some Africans to adapt to. In Lubumbashi, when a well-dressed white man approached a sidewalk shoeshine stand, meaning to be the next patron after a well-dressed Congolese in the chair, the African leaped up to yield his place; it was the old *bwana* syndrome at work. I myself was several times called "Master"—once, outlandishly, on the steps leading to a fortress on the Guinea coast where slaves awaiting transshipment were imprisoned. I was thus addressed so often that I felt almost relieved to experience the reverse: When I presented myself one day at the outer office of the External Affairs Ministry of Nigeria and requested to be announced to the official with whom I had an appointment, the receptionist did not bother to look at my card or ask for my name, but instead merely passed the word inside that waiting outside was "One European."

In black Africa today, one's whiteness provokes little overt truculence. Once on Gorée Island, that bleak Senegalese outpost whence other slaves embarked for America, a class from the University of Dakar came by, notebooks in hand, and one African student inquired in French about my nationality. "*Les Etats Unis*," I said in the vernacular. He shifted into English, and, apparently trying to make me feel uncomfortable, said with heavy sarcasm, "Welcome to the gateway to Alabama." And outside a hotel in Monrovia, there was the burly Liberian who, when I tried to dissuade him from squeezing into a taxi that already had five white passengers in it, muttered, "Oh, so you don't like Africans!" But he was very drunk. Whiteness is not yet scorned *per se* in black Africa. The promotional brochure for that same Liberian hotel is illustrated with far more photographs of white folks than of black, and the blacks depicted are quite light-skinned. (Throughout West Africa, one sees billboards touting Satina skin-whitener.) In some of the francophone countries of West Africa quite a few ranking Africans still have, and are seemingly none the worse off politically for, white French wives. Nevertheless, there are indications here and there that white skin is no longer venerated. In a number of countries, if Africans see one African rob another, and if they can catch the culprit before the police do, they are apt to beat him to death. In a Dakar supermarket, by contrast, several African onlookers merely shrugged when a white French boy snatched a white Frenchwoman's purse.

One can hardly begin to look at emerging Africa these days without a backward glance at the submerged Kwame Nkrumah. The once glorious and vainglorious Osagyefo—liberator of Ghana (née Gold Coast), prospective ruler of his chimerical Union of West African Socialist Republics—sits brooding now in Sekou Touré's Guinea, an enclave lately inaccessible to most Westerners except Stokely Carmichael. During the Portuguese-inspired, if not -conducted, invasion of Guinea in November, 1970, the raiders bypassed Nkrumah's residence, apparently not considering it worth even a passing fusillade; back in Accra, where his splashy monuments still pop the eye, one newspaper tartly commented, "Such are the blessings of obscurity."

A fallen mighty man Nkrumah may be now, but it was he perhaps more than any other individual who sparked the blaze of African independence. In Ghana, he broke the tribal chieftains' strangling feudal power and substituted an up-to-date political structure before he became, like some other contemporary African politicians, too corrupt and too ambitious for his own, or his country's, good. One of Nkrumah's failings was that, dreaming of continental unity, he lost track of more immediate concerns. He kept trying to be Mr. Pan-Africa at a time when he was barely on speaking terms with his immediate neighbors. The African political scientist Ali Mazrui has sad that "while Nkrumah strived to be Africa's Lenin, he also sought to be Ghana's Czar." Seduced by autocracy, Nkrumah lost his touch and the trust of his people; shortly before his downfall, in 1966, he who earlier had freely talked to his fellow Ghanaians from his bathtub was isolated from them by iron gates and hard-eyed thugs. To be sure, the CIA was accused of helping to plot his overthrow, which occurred on the day he arrived in Peking from Hanoi, still pursuing far-off alliances. But the CIA gets blamed for just about everything that goes wrong in Africa. The *Legon Observer*, a scholarly journal put out at the University of Ghana, not long ago declared editorially, "When an oppressive regime becomes unbearable, the local people usually find a way of getting rid of it—as happened in Ghana, even though in our case an incredulous world still believes that outsiders had a hand in it." (The *Observer* is not above incredulousness itself; the same issue carried an article about the United States, a country credited "with police facilities which can take a sample of the urine of any Head of State or of Government they choose to, any day.")

For all Nkrumah's flaws, though, he may have been the ideal man for his time. The perceptive Taban Lo Liyong has said, "Rather than ask whether Nkrumah had not failed us, we should ask if we, his dream, have not failed him, whether we have not failed to sustain that noble dream." Whatever else Nkrumah did or was or dreamed, he gave the African independence movement the impetus it needed at a critical juncture. "Seek ye first the political kingdom, and all things shall be added to it," he once wrote. He sought and found that realm, but he seemed incapable of augmenting it. From his deposal, and the toppling of some other leaders and the shakiness of still more, some thoughtful Africans have surmised that perhaps on their continent each country needs two successive George Washingtons—one to attain independence and the other to make it work. To proponents of this theory, some of the recent untidy changes of government in independent Africa have been not so much revolutionary in nature as part of an evolutionary process. The fact is that by worldwide standards most Africans are not very radical. For all their pronouncements about the socialistic way of life, what is more likely than anything else to deter them from a convulsive swing to the left—no matter how much the bumbling or indifferent West may sometimes seem to wish to push them there—is that most of them are subsistence-agriculture people only lately exposed to the bewitchments of a money economy, and more than anything else they would like to become capitalists.

The 1960s, now sometimes called the Decade of Disappointment, were the years of political development for black Africa. Now Africans are starting in on their Decade of Economic Development—they hope. Ten years ago, they had a pie-in-the-sky attitude toward prosperity (one of the incongruities of contemporary Africa is that although hardly anyone eats pie, everyone talks about wanting a larger piece of it); now they are becoming more realistic about their prospects and are looking to their political leaders for economic guidance. Here again Nkrumah unwittingly taught Africa a lesson: It does not follow that economic stability will come under the stewardship of the same leaders who have brought about political freedom. The visionary, the exhorter, the eloquent declaimer of dreams, may be terrible at coping with a budget. Nkrumah might still be in power had he, among other things, elected to concentrate on developing his country's agriculture, inasmuch as agriculture was, and is, Africa's chief enterprise. It is the principal occupation of six and a half of Ghana's eight million people. But no, Nkrumah wanted to jump straight into the modern world. He spent huge sums on huge buildings, including one in Accra known, from its contractor's number, as "Job 600." It cost some twenty-five million dollars and was to have been a permanent encampment for African summit conferences. It had apartments for every head of state, some of these fitted out with six-foot-high balcony walls, so that the occupants couldn't readily be sniped at. (Unless they were a good deal taller than Emperor Haile Selassie, they couldn't see out, either.) Because of Nkrumah's lavish investments in the appurtenances of rank and glory, Ghanaians ruefully say today that they have the world's largest surplus of flagpoles. They also have an anguished Italian sculptor on their necks, an artist who did a one-and-a-half-times lifesize statue of Nkrumah for display outside Parliament House, and who just before the Osagyefo's dismissal received a firm commission from him to execute eight more in the same heroic proportions.

While Nkrumah was at it, he embarked on some manufacturing schemes that sounded impressive and had the added attraction of providing nearly everybody involved in them with a nice source of graft. There was a mango-processing factory, for one, with a projected annual output of more than a thousand tons of mango preserves. But after the plant was built it developed that the entire global demand for mango preserves amounted only to something like fifty tons a year, and besides, the factory had been built at a spot where there were no mango trees. Still, it was difficult to denounce such ventures in the first hot flush of independence. Anyone who did was apt to be denounced himself as an old-fashioned colonial type bent on stifling African imagination. Today, the mango factory stands moribund, and Ghana is in a dreadful economic fix. Because of money borrowed during the Nkrumah regime, the incumbent government, despite three re-negotiations of its debts to other nations, has to make annual payments on outstanding loans that come to just about fifty per cent of all the foreign aid funds it receives.

Nkrumah was by no means the only African leader to go in for flashy, costly architecture, with all the trimmings. Liberia's William V. S. Tubman had a sixteen-million-dollar Presidential palace in Monrovia, and the visitors' reception chamber in the Liberian foreign office looks like a cross between a Versailles throne room and a California funeral parlor. The best roads in Africa are likely to be those that lead from a capital city to the rural residence of the chief of state. Plain vanity is not the only reason for these displays of opulence amid glaring poverty. African leaders who evolved from colonialism are partial to extravagances, Professor Mazrui has said, because "there are certain forms of humiliation which, when ended, give rise to flamboyant self-assertion."

For all their expressed devotion to the aspirations of the common man, most of the leaders of black Africa are elitists, and they constitute a sort of club, informal but exclusive. Nkrumah found a haven in Guinea partly because when Sekou Touré desperately needed financial help after independence and had nowhere else to turn, Ghana came through with twelve million dollars. But that wasn't the only reason. They were both members of the club. For years before Nkrumah's downfall he hadn't been detectably friendly with another neighbor, the comparatively conservative Félix Houphouët-Boigny of Ivory Coast; yet Houphouët-Boigny asserts today that if he'd been asked he would certainly have granted Nkrumah sanctuary, just as he was to do for a somewhat less tenured club member, Odumegwu Ojukwu of Biafra, who ever since his bubble burst has been in residence at Yamassoukro, Houphouët-Boigny's birthplace and rural retreat. (The highway north from Abidjan, the Ivorian capital, is paved as far as Yamassoukro and no farther.)

Houphouët-Boigny, probably black Africa's most successful conservative leader, likes to tell how his course diverged from Nkrumah's. "In 1957, Nkrumah was my best friend," the Ivorian says. "We came from the same tribe, and spoke the same dialect. We were separated only by the circumstances of colonialism. When the Ivory Coast became independent, I said to him, 'You are ahead of us now. We haven't a sou. But I'll bet you that in ten years we'll be ahead of you.' Unhappily, he took a path different from ours, and things didn't work out for him. But we would have given him a home if he had asked. In Africa, one must even sustain one's enemy. We have no room here for the politics of vengeance and hate."

The African leaders enjoy getting together, when they have

freedom of movement, in the manner of old-school-tie chums anywhere, and not merely at formal gatherings like summit conferences of the Organization of African Unity, nor even merely for
bilateral state visits, though these are frequent and protracted.
Many of the African leaders are well acquainted because they have
been around and in charge for quite a while. Despite the belief
outside of Africa that its heads of state, voluntarily or involuntarily, are forever playing musical chairs, most of the leaders of
consequence have had respectable incumbencies. Their longevity
in office has earned them high protocolary standing. At General
de Gaulle's funeral, Richard Nixon, not even a two-year president,
had to take a back seat to half a dozen African chiefs of state,
preeminent among whom, of course, was Haile Selassie, the No. 1
man on everybody's protocol list.

It is probably a fairly safe generalization that all Africans have
a considerable respect, if not reverence, for rooted authority—in
tribe, in church, in school, in state—and this is nowhere more
evident than in Ethiopia, where His Imperial Majesty is often
known by the simple acronymic word "HIM"; where in a campus
production of *Julius Caesar* the assassination scene was omitted, as
unsuitable for local consumption; and where the newspapers, such
as they are, avoid running stories of manifestations of discontent
with authority anywhere, be it Washington, Moscow, Freetown,
Yaounde, or, it goes without saying, Addis Ababa. An editor in
Addis told me, "We feel sentimental toward any leader who's been
on the scene for a long time." In Liberia, where the late President
Tubman governed so long that he was sometimes called, though
not in print, "the only hereditary elected president in the world,"
the papers treated him with idolatry. A typical headline proclaimed:
"President Tubman's Annual Message Hailed By All! They Say
It's Straight Forward, Frank, And Progressive!" A typical editorial
went, "It is now clear that Dr. Tubman is a real Leader whose
foresight is beyond imagination."

There is some grumbling among African students about per-
sonality cultism, but not much, for as young people go they are
on the whole quite muted and circumspect. Besides, they are as
quick as Africans of any age to embrace, uncritically, a new
leader. It sometimes puzzles outsiders how rapidly an African

25

country seems to revert to normal after a coup. One reason may be the undiscriminating admiration of authority figures. An African audience will loudly cheer one leader's speech one day and the next day as loudly cheer a speech the opposite in content, if it is uttered by a man of suitable stature. Just before independence, indeed, Africans were cheering the speeches of colonial governors.

Adulation is as much a part of the African landscape as the thorn bush or market place. African presidents may sometimes need bodyguards to protect them against their own armed forces, but not ordinarily against their idolatrous people. When Jomo Kenyatta takes a drive around Mombasa, his path is cleared by motorcycle cops who wave other cars to the edge of the road, and if the drivers have time they hop out and bow low as the Mzee's Mercedes sweeps by. When Haile Selassie inspects a new library, the stack boys prostrate themselves before him, and even some Americans, after a few years' residence in Ethiopia, have found that the approach of the Lion of Judah inspires them to thoughts of genuflection.

The popularity of the entrenched leaders is emphatically indicated by the votes they receive—in those countries, that is, where elections are held. When Houphouët-Boigny last ran for president, he got 99.19 percent of the vote. In the Congo, President Joseph Mobutu's most recent percentage was 99.97. In Tanzania, President Nyerere had to settle for 98.79 percent. These were one-slate elections, to be sure, but the lack of opposition does not disturb African leaders. Houphouët-Boigny, a strong advocate of participatory politics—"To vote is an obligation," said one election poster in Abidjan; "it is to build the nation"—insists further that university applicants join the only extant political party in Ivory Coast (his party) before they matriculate. He feels that a one-party setup is defensible because for young nations with hardly any unifying traditions—with, rather, long histories of tribal wars conducive to fragmentation—it would be foolish to tolerate, let alone encourage, multiparty politics. Any country that did might end up with a party for every tribe within its boundaries, and some countries have hundreds of tribes. Moreover, an exposure to political alternatives might be not only foolish but fatal to the leaders themselves, some of whom even without lawful oppositions act as if they were gazelles ringed by hyenas.

In a country like the United States, any candidate who garnered eighty percent of a vote would deduce that he was in by a landslide and would look confidently toward the future. In Africa today, any candidate who failed to get twenty percent of a vote would deduce that he was on the skids and look warily over his shoulder. Yet it took hundreds of years, in the western world, for such refined political institutions as parliaments with built-in oppositions to become acceptable. Heads of governments in Africa—many of whom, under colonialism, were leaders of outlawed parties themselves—find it difficult this early in the game to work with, or even abide, oppositions. From their own experience, they tend to equate opposition with subversion. So they declare rivalry illegal. Africans who nonetheless publicly stand up against an incumbent are likely to be considered his enemy, and in Africa it has long been the practice to dispose of one's enemies firmly—by detention if one is feeling benevolent or, if one is annoyed, by something worse. Tanzania, a country genuinely devoted to improving the human condition, doesn't have a Bill of Rights in its Constitution. "We thought about having a Bill, like Kenya, but we decided against it in the light of our being a one-party state," a government man told me in Dar es Salaam. "As a practical matter, a Bill of Rights is ineffective in a developing country. The only way to guarantee human rights is to have an acceptance of the ethic that lies behind them. If you have that, you don't need a bill. And if you don't have it, any bill you do have can be circumvented by a government with an overwhelming parliamentary majority, since it can always amend the Constitution. That sort of action leads to cynicism. And Africa has already absorbed about as much cynicism as it can stand."

2

There are forty-one independent countries in Africa. Not long ago there were just two—Ethiopia and Liberia. There is nothing magical about the number "forty-one" and no reason to assume it will be a political constant: after all, stamp collectors specializing in African issues (the smallest countries, like Burundi and Togo, inevitably issue the biggest number of varieties) have Biafra pages in their 1968 and 1969 volumes. Some political scientists believe that the nations that emerged between 1957 and 1964 can more or less be fitted into one of three categories. First, there are those that because of size, location, natural resources, and quality of leadership—among them, Nigeria, Kenya, the Ivory Coast, Tanzania, and perhaps Congo (Kinshasa), now Zaire—would seem to be almost certain of surviving. Second, there are those—Ghana, Uganda, Senegal, Liberia, Sierra Leone, and others—that seem slightly more likely than not to make a go of it. And then there are those that could cease to exist at any time without causing much surprise—such as Rwanda, Dahomey, Niger, Upper Volta, and Congo (Brazzaville)—because they are small, volatile, and poor; it sometimes seems that their only raison d'être is that they do exist.

However one classifies the lot of them, nearly all of them are beset by some shared problems. Two of these are the high rise in population and the low rise in literacy. Between 1900 and 1930, the population of Africa—which for all its size, four times that of the United States, is inhabited today by merely three hundred and fifty million people—climbed at a rate of six-tenths of one percent a year. By the early 1960s, the rate was nearly two and a half percent. Now, in some of the equatorial countries, it is undoubtedly higher than three percent, though there is no certainty about most African statistics. The population of Nigeria, for instance, is somewhere between sixty and eighty million (the government claims sixty-six), but no one knows for sure. A recent census was a fiasco; the government announced in advance that it would be used to determine the allocation of federal funds and jobs to the several regions of the country, and most regions played so loose with the figures they submitted to Lagos that all the data were thrown away. Offhand, it would seem that giant Africa could accommodate limitless numbers of people, but this is not the case. Much of the land is worthless for crops, and not much better for grazing; of the two hundred and thirty thousand square miles of Kenya, to cite just one instance, a mere thirty thousand have any agricultural potentiality. And the surge of breeding that has paralleled independence has resulted in a population imbalance: Some forty-five percent of all Africans are under fifteen; thus while they are consumers they contribute very little in productivity to their societies.

It is no surprise, then, that many Africans have lately begun to think hard about birth control. It is a touchy subject, because any infringement on natural procreation runs counter to the doctrines of many African churches and conflicts also with the extended-family system that is so prevalent across the continent. Many Africans are relaxed about sex, illegitimacy is no stigma, and high infant mortality is supposed to keep everything in balance. Unfortunately—in a demographic sense—the outside world has come to Africa's assistance much more effectively with death control than with birth control. African women who a generation ago could expect only one or two surviving children from eight births can now anticipate that five or six will live. In fifteen countries today—as opposed to none four years ago—there are family planning groups of one sort or another, but their clinics do not always serve their stated purpose; the women who go to them sometimes want help in planning *larger* families, and doctors and nurses assigned to dispense contraceptives instead find themselves handing out fertility pills. (If a birth-control injection were developed, it could profoundly alter the pattern of African life, for many Africans love shots; some consider a visit to a doctor wasted unless they get one. During the cholera epidemic that swept eastward along the Equator at the end of 1970, killing at least fifteen thousand people, free inoculations were offered on the streets of Niamey, the capital of Niger, and it was reported that some people got in line half a dozen times for the pure pleasure of being jabbed.)

It is difficult to get the birth-control message across to people who are accustomed to living contentedly with swarms of children and whose austere residential habits make adequate living space no problem. Ghana has been notably resolute among the emerging nations in urging limitations on families. The Prime Minister's wife is chairman of the National Family Planning Council there, and the increase in births has been declining a bit. But at the same time the incidence of child-stealing has increased by more than one hundred and fifty percent. The propaganda has to be tailored to suit the locality. A family-planning group produced a documentary film for the Yoruba tribe of western Nigeria. Because the Yorubas are talk-oriented and habitually get much of their news from orations, the movie had little action and nearly an hour of speechifying. It went over so well that it was later shown, with an appropriate sound track, to some Kikuyus in Kenya, who get much of their news through gossip. They found it a bore.

Above all, no matter how suitably or delicately the message is couched, its transmitters try not to make it seem as though family planning was something devised by whites to curb the propagation of blacks. For the birth-control movement (the actual words "birth control" are scrupulously avoided) to acquire overtones of genocide could be, as family-planning proponents have learned in the United States and elsewhere, discomfiting if not disastrous. Not long ago, the International Planned Parenthood Federation

31

prepared for distribution in Africa a folder that featured a photograph of an African mother smiling tenderly at an infant. "This woman has a new baby," the caption said. "What happens if she gets pregnant again when the first baby is only this size?" The reaction of several Africans who saw it was tart. Why did people who complained of population explosions always fortify their arguments with *black* illustrations, they demanded. Why not show a picture of a *white* child and suggest that there were enough of his kind on earth? The folder was withdrawn. The most prudent, and most effective, argument that birth-control advocates have found so far in Africa is the economic one that if parents are obliged to share their material resources with a whole flock of offspring, they'll presumably have less to enjoy themselves.

Even if someone were to compose an overwhelmingly compelling tract in favor of African population control, it couldn't make much headway among the people for whom it was designed, because few of them could read it. The end of colonialism did not automatically presage the start of literacy. Ethiopia has been independent the longest of any African nation, but Ethiopia is still ninety percent illiterate, unless one counts as literate those people who have been taught enough Amharic by the Coptic Church to follow the Scriptures, in which case the figure can be reduced to about eighty-three percent. Ethiopia has lately embarked on a drive to promote literacy, and the government asserts that fifty thousand people are now learning to read and write each year; but that represents slightly less than two percent of the population, and the increase in the birth rate there is slightly *more* than two percent a year.

The outlook is depressing wherever one turns. In Liberia, the second oldest independent nation, one-third of the population has never gone to school. There is ninety-five percent illiteracy in northern Nigeria, and ninety-five percent in Senegal—though its president is the very literate poet Leopold Sedar-Senghor, who in 1971 received an honorary degree from Harvard. In Ghana, the first of the emerging nations, with, moreover, a tradition of education stretching back for a century or more, a new girls' school called the Paradise Vocational College opened at the start of 1971 with the announcement that it had vacancies for two kinds of students—literate and illiterate. The Ivory Coast hopes by the year 1981 to have a huge new tourist facility completed at Abidjan; it also hopes, with less confidence, to have attained universal literacy by that date. Meanwhile, each country struggles after its own fashion to raise the levels of comprehension and communication of its inhabitants (making do in the interim with some hotel clerks who cannot read envelopes and taxi drivers who cannot read maps). A journalist in Abidjan told me that he found his job especially taxing because if he were writing an article in a country like the United States, where ninety percent of the population can read with relative ease, it would take him twenty minutes; but to write so that even ten percent of his fellow countrymen can follow his words takes him three hours.

The spread of the written word in Africa is further impeded by the sheer physical difficulty of transporting anything at all from place to place. Few as the literates are in Ethiopia, it might be expected that in that country of nearly twenty-five million the principal newspaper would have a circulation larger than seventeen thousand. But it doesn't, in part because more than eighty percent of the population lives more than a full day's march from a road of any sort. Even in as relatively up-to-date a country as the Ivory Coast, it takes a newspaper two days to get from Abidjan to the northern border, 350 miles away; to expedite deliveries closer to the capital city, the publisher of the principal daily, the *Fraternité-Matin*, arranged for taxis to carry copies on their suburban runs, but it is hard to get most cab-drivers anywhere interested in other peoples' problems, and deliveries were slipshod.

Much as contemporary Africa reveres independence, it does not hold in equally high esteem the independence of the press. Fifty-one percent of the stock of the *Fraternité-Matin*, typically, belongs to the Ivory Coast government; the paper never criticizes the government except over such minor issues as the degree of diligence of post-office clerks. The editor, a smart, suave Ivorian of thirty named Laurent Dona-Fologo, who received his academic and journalistic training in France, is also a member of the governing body of Houphouët-Boigny's political party. Dona-Fologo regularly has confidential talks with the president, and construes it to be part of his editorial function to explain presidential actions.

33

The editor is not nagged by concerns over conflicts of interest. "I only write what I believe," he says. But he reserves the right—with the prudence displayed by many an African editor these days —not to put all his beliefs in writing. The restraints that he imposes on himself seem to him not imcompatible with the ideals of his profession. "In underdeveloped countries there is never total liberty," he told me. "The people are still too susceptible and emotional and don't have lucid judgment. So we don't give them everything."

The press tends to be more discreet in those countries that used to be French colonies and in most instances retain close ties to their former masters. The staff of Le Soleil, the Dakar daily, is predominantly French, not Senegalese; and when the President of Senegal holds a press conference, it is observed custom that only the French journalists in attendance ask questions. There is far more diversity and dissent in the former British colonies. When Ghana became independent, twenty-three daily papers at once sprang up in Accra, most of them short-lived. That capital city, though, still usually has at any given time about three dailies, six semi-weeklies, and three or four Sunday papers. The dissent has its limitations; a journalist can get fired for writing a single editorial that displeases the government, and one newspaper reporter I met—a man who had been detained some months earlier for disputing the official government version that the President of Ghana, then in London, was suffering from gout and for disclosing the truth that he had suffered a stroke—told me that he was using a borrowed typewriter because the police, subjecting him to periodic harassment, had been around a few days earlier and had taken away his own machine. "I told the police that they couldn't silence me," the reporter said, "but that only God could, by taking away my breath, and one of the cops said to me, 'You must be a brave man,' and I replied, 'Yes, the truth feareth not.'" Africans talk like that when they get emotional.

Nigeria, another former British colony, has some seventy newspapers, a fairly respectable one-paper-per-million-residents ratio, and some of these are rather outspoken, though many of them are subsidized, to one degree or another, by either the Nigerian or the British government. Most of the editors go to jail every now and then, but this is commonplace in Africa; the editor of *Le Progrès*, the leading paper in Kinshasa, considers it evidential of the comparative freedom of the press enjoyed in Zaire that he has been imprisoned only once. He, too, believes in circumspection; he, too, often confers with his president, and does not much take him to task. But then these editors are after all Africans, and share with other Africans the continent-wide respect for authority.

There is only one really important rule for journalists in Kenya, and it is unwritten and self-imposed: Under no circumstances may the president be criticized in print. And although everybody knows Jomo Kenyatta is over eighty and although the identity of his successor as the chief regional authority figure is much on the minds of every Kenyan whose concerns extend beyond his own local hearth, the question of presidential succession is never mentioned in the press, either directly or by implication.

Every so often, however, a fretful African journalist just cannot resist taking a potshot at a sacrosanct target. In an election campaign speech in 1967, President Tubman (who in an earlier contest once received 530,566 votes to an opponent's 55) said that the government was going to take action against the writers of anonymous letters of complaint and used the phrase "The net is closing in." Reporting on a similar pre-election speech of his four years later, in his last walkover before his death, one daring paper put that phrase in a headline, even though this time Tubman hadn't used the words; the idea was to remind readers, subtly, that this was more of the old routine campaign hokum. But it was so oblique an allusion that scarcely anyone got the point.

After I had spent five weeks in tropical West Africa, my first East African stop was Entebbe, Uganda. I drove from there to the capital, Kampala, with an educated Ugandan who along the way interrupted our conversation to inform me that the plants at the edge of the road were banana trees. Yes, I said, I knew; as *he* knew, I had just concluded more than a month's stay in West Africa. "Oh," my companion said, surprised, "do they grow bananas there, too?" A couple of weeks earlier, when I had asked a hotel desk clerk in Accra to post a letter to Bujumbura, Burundi, he had asked where this Burundi was, and when he learned it was a full-fledged African nation, *he* had been surprised. If East Africa and West Africa know so little about each other, it is perhaps not surprising that most of the rest of the world is so ignorant about both of them.

Independence came first to West Africa, mainly because that region, though much earlier explored by the outside world, had acquired fewer settlers who could logically be expected to resent and resist displacement. Kenya, in East Africa, was (aside from the *sui generis* South Africa) where most of the permanent British residents chose to stay, largely owing to its cool, dry highlands; but there were no British at all in Kenya till the turn of the twentieth century, a decade after Kenyatta was born. There are quite a few Kenyans, Ugandans, and Tanzanians around who can remember the first white man they ever saw. At about the same time that the first female Kenyan entered a secondary school, Nigeria already had two hundred members in its Federation of Women Lawyers.

In West Africa, women have long been a political force to reckon with. They dominate the marketplaces. They speak their piece in no uncertain tones. No politician can hope to get far without courting their support. In East Africa, even though some individual women have risen high in politics, they are not much listened to en bloc; there, a politician whose wife was overheard talking back to him in public couldn't hope to get elected to anything. (African women everywhere are clearly enjoying the new relationships between the races as much as African men are; to sense this, one need merely watch the facial expressions as two white British males sit stolidly in an automobile in Nairobi while two black policewomen meticulously write out a traffic ticket.)

Europeans were conspicuous in West Africa nearly half a millennium before they settled in the East. It is widely believed that Columbus explored Africa the year before he discovered America. But the Europeans didn't put down deep West African roots. They couldn't tolerate the malarial rain forests along the Gulf of Guinea, which became known, with good reason, as the White Man's Grave. The Prime Minister of Sierra Leone told a visitor not long ago that a fitting symbol for his country's coat of arms could be the mosquito. Asked why, he replied, "It kept the settlers out."

West Africa has a richer history than the East. Most of the best African music and dancing and art come from the West. (An employee of Ghana's national museum, in Accra, offered one day to escort me to a place—the home of a friend of his—where I could buy some first-rate pieces; when I mentioned this later to one of the curators, he said he'd like very much to receive such an invitation himself, inasmuch as a number of the museum's better pieces were missing.) Not only are the West Africans, by and large, more creative than the Easterners, they are livelier. They wear brighter colors, they are more prone to dance and laugh, they are more relaxed, they seem to have more fun. A Zambian's idea of dressing up is to don a dark sack suit; a Ghanaian's, to wear a dazzling robe. When Kenya achieved its independence, there was appropriate jubilation in Nairobi, and a West African who happened to be visiting marveled at the comparatively subdued atmosphere; when, the next day, the city's stores opened for business as usual, he shook his head and told a Kenyan acquaintance, "If this were happening in *my* part of Africa, we'd all be drunk for a week." The very names of the stores in East and West Africa reflect the differences in *joie de vivre*. In Kenya, one sees brisk, businesslike names like "Guns and Cameras," in Ghana freewheeling ones like the "Why Worry Records and Blouse Store," the "Life Is a Game Store," or—this last a tailor shop—the "Ever Happy Fitting Brothers." It is not uncommon, in Accra, to come upon a perfectly sober Ghanaian singing aloud while walking along a street; such carryings-on in Kampala or Lusaka would be taken as evidence of, at the very least, unconventionality.

Foreigners who tend to make sport of Africa are partial to the acronym "Wawa." It stands for "West Africa wins again." "Wawa" is a kind of safety valve; it is supposed to be muttered to one's self or one's foreign companion when a West African does or says something ludicrous, inconveniencing, or infuriating. There is no comparable acronym for East Africa, which in the eyes of the Wawaists is on the whole a less hilarious region; besides, "Eawa" doesn't have a haha ring to it. Eawa exists, all right; an example of

37

it would be the Nairobi bank teller who stubbornly insisted, despite all appeals to experience and common sense, that a visitor who wanted to buy some travelers' checks should make out his personal check not to the bank but to the visitor himself.

Like everyone else who has been to West Africa, I have my own dossier of Wawa stories. There is a brief entry on the hotel doorman in Nigeria who, asked to summon a taxi, said, "But you had one yesterday." There is a paragraph dedicated to the secretary of the Liberian government minister with whom I had a twelve-thirty appointment. After I had arrived on time and waited ten minutes, the secretary said he was very sorry but the minister was all tied up, and could I return at twelve-thirty? When I pointed out that it was already twelve-forty and added that I hoped I wouldn't have to wait too much longer because I had a lunch date with another minister at one-thirty, the secretary said that in that case, since *his* minister wouldn't be leaving his office until two, why didn't I come back after lunch? But these were trivial experiences; what struck me more than the omnipresence of Wawa was its infrequency; I have encountered as much Wawa in western America—in California, come to think of it, perhaps more—as in western Africa.

In the forefront of most Wawa anthologies are breathless accounts of the helter-skelter operating methods of African airlines (the pilots are principally European), as if one could reasonably count on split-second adherence to schedules everywhere else on earth. There is a certain picaresqueness about African airlines. Most of them are owned by governments, or by consortiums of governments, and high officials of the states whose colors they bear sometimes commandeer planes impulsively. Air Congo passengers may end up somewhere other than their destination if a cabinet minister is aboard their flight and, wanting to get to Kinshasa as quickly as possible, orders the pilot to skip Bujumbura or some other scheduled intermediate stop. I was delayed five hours one day when the President of Uganda took over an East African Airways flight for his own devices. Ghana Airways is thought by most connoisseurs of Wawa, and by not a few Ghanaians, too, to be the most bizarre. While I was in Accra, the papers there complained that the airline's passengers "are left stranded sometimes without any explanation at all." Just before traveling by Ghana Airways from Abidjan to Accra, I heard of a grotesque series of misadventures that befell an American tour group traveling across West Africa on Ghanaian wings—overbookings, canceled flights, inexplicable delays, and lost luggage. But my own flight was right on time and completely uneventful. Indeed, it is the uneventfulness of much of one's experiences in independent Africa that, when one is trying to assess the progress of black self-government, sometimes seems most eventful.

3

In their quest for economic independence, Africans are increasingly thinking in regional terms. This is scarcely a novel continental concept. The colonialists espoused it. The British had some common services in West Africa and in East Africa had even more. Since 1958, the Economic Commission for Africa, a United Nations agency that operates out of Addis Ababa, has been trying, without breathtaking success, to persuade its member states that their main hope for economic advancement lies in regional or subregional cooperation. Since independence, Africa has seen the birth of so many regional groups that even full-time Africanists are sometimes hard-pressed to keep them all straight. There is the Entente Africaine, a francophone group in West Africa consisting of Togo, Dahomey, Niger, Upper Volta, and the Ivory Coast. Ghana, except where it touches the sea, is surrounded by it on all sides, but Ghana, being an anglophone nation, does not belong to it. Another francophone ensemble is the Central African Customs and Economic Union (Cameroon, Gabon, Congo (Brazzaville), and the Central African Republic). Still another is the fifteen-nation Afro-Malagasy Common Organization, generally known as OCAM. Guinea is not a member, and President Sekou Touré sometimes twittingly refers to this one as the *"Organisation Contre Afrique en Marche."*

The late President Tubman thought a couple of years ago that he had a fourteen-nation organization in the making that would have included both anglophone and francophone states, but it never got under way because the Ivory Coast, which dominates the Entente Africaine, stayed out and—according to Liberia—also somehow saw to it that when delegates from Dahomey and Togo stopped off at Abidjan en route to an organizational meeting at Monrovia, the transportation they'd counted on to take them the rest of the way mysteriously vanished. The Ivory Coast, moreover, plays a key regional role because Abidjan has become the head-quarters both of the eleven-nation Air Afrique (it was a twelve-nation airline until Cameroon defected, claiming it employed too few Cameroonians), and of the African Development Bank, a pan-African institution that has been functioning, on a limited scale, since 1966. When the Bank is in full swing, it expects to have capital funds of two hundred and fifty million dollars. These are to be furnished, according to their capabilities, by its thirty-two member nations. The minimum assessment is one million, a sum that for small members like Malawi, Niger, and Rwanda has proved hard to raise. To be eligible for membership, a country must further be "independent and developing." The Republic of South Africa, which could easily put up the ante, has been excluded—not that it probably cares one way or the other—because most of the rest of Africa doesn't consider its black residents to be independent or developing. In its first five years, the Bank loaned a total of twenty-five million dollars, for such ventures as an irrigation project in Tunisia, a gas turbine in Liberia, a paper mill in Kenya, and a water system in Sierra Leone. It matched that sum in 1971 alone. The bank is managed, and its grants approved, exclusively by Africans. "This bank is a sort of act of faith to show that Africans can run their own affairs—and fiscal affairs in particular," one of the officers told me.

One hindrance to an orderly economic development of independent Africa has been an uneven distribution of natural resources. Africa is rich in minerals, many of them as yet unexploited, but some countries have much more subsurface wealth than others, and some have none at all. And of the resources, natural or cultivated, that have so far proved marketable, a number of nations have proved to be perilously dependent on the world demand and world price for a single product—peanuts in Senegal, palm oil in Dahomey, coffee in Burundi, copper in Zambia, and so forth.

Perhaps an even more serious deterrent to the kind of economic advancement most of Africa would like to see, and enjoy, is the basic incompatibility between the necessity of regional associations and the surges of national pride that independence has understandably evoked. Nationalism inhibits progress in all areas: Togo and Dahomey were to have a joint university, which would have made sense, since between them they have only four and a half million people and precious few assets, but then they couldn't get together on details, so now each little country is spending more than it can afford on its own institution. A separate university, however inferior academically it may be to a joint one, at least—like a separate international airline—fosters national pride.

The search for status symbols goes on unabatedly in Africa. In the economic area, three of the most popular these days are an oil refinery, a tire factory, and a cement plant. The Ivory Coast could with its existing facilities readily supply all the cement Dahomey could conceivably use, but no matter, Dahomey is determined to have its own plant and to produce its own Dahomeyan cement from its own rather poor-quality limestone. It would seem logical for Liberia, rich in rubber, to manufacture tires and sell them to the Ivory Coast, which in turn could provide Liberia with all the textiles it requires. But the Ivory Coast must have its own tire plant, just as Liberia, which could efficiently fill its requirements for flour from Sierra Leone, is determined to have a mill of its own.

Africans like to talk about unity, and intellectually they know they need it to make economic headway, but emotionally they often shy away from it. Indeed, at the same time that—often, alas, at arm's length—they embrace internationalism, they are beset at home merely to preserve the spirit of nationalism. "The theoretical dilemma seems acute," Professor Mazrui has written. "Tribalism can only be conquered at the cost of pan-Africanism—or so it painfully appears." Nkrumah, the original pan-Africanist, had lessened the impact of tribalism on Ghana, but as time went by, and the heady glow of nationalism cooled, there has been, if anything, a resurgence of tribalism. An editorial in an Accra paper deploring the prevalence of theft did not call upon the central government to take preventive steps but, rather, said that the "chiefs should cause the gong-gong to be beaten to explain the seriousness of the situation to their people."

There are close to one thousand distinct tribes south of the Sahara. Nigeria alone has two hundred and fifty of them, and the Ivory Coast, with only four million inhabitants, harbors sixty definable ethnic divisions. Moreover, most Africans, whatever their national fealties, are ever conscious of their tribal origins. Ask many an urbanized African where his home is, and he may reply not with his residential address but the seat of his tribe. Some viewers of the African scene have suggested that the smaller countries, though frail and feeble by almost any measurements, are in a sense better off than some of their big neighbors simply because they have fewer tribes. (On the other hand, they may have grave *sectional* problems; in Dahomey, most of the northern upland people, regardless of their tribal affiliations, are unanimous in their distaste for most of southern coastal people, regardless of *theirs*.)

Some of the heads of state in Africa have been trying of late to play down the tribal rivalries that can be so disruptive. In Zambia, where tribalism has recently been the single most important reason for political unrest, President Kaunda has forbidden allusions to its existence in the newspapers; at the same time his Ministry of Information has a map, not for public circulation, showing the tribal divisions within that country. It looks like a crazy quilt. In Kenya, the very essence of national politics is and long has been tribal, and tribalism figures equally importantly on the social scene. (Only in certain economic areas is tribalism inconsequential; an unemployed Kikuyu can sound off just as bitterly at the predominantly Kikuyu government as an unemployed Luo or anyone else.) Most Kenyans, however educated, however worldly, however well-traveled, wouldn't dream of marrying across tribal lines. I met one couple in Nairobi who fell in love while they were at a university in England. They were both Luos and were desperately eager to wed at once, but they postponed their marriage for two years, until they had completed their studies, for it would have been unthinkable in their view for them to take the step without being inspected by their respective relatives and without going through other tribal formalities. They expected their children, what was more, to conform to tribal custom when they get married, including the prenuptial delivery, by a prospective bridegroom, of an appropriate number of cattle. When I asked the couple if there was any *legal* reason why a Kenyan couldn't marry anyone he chose to, they looked at each other and then looked at me and the wife said gently, "In Kenya, and in Africa, the laws that are never broken are those that are never written."

The emphasis on nationalism as an antidote to tribalism has produced a backlash of sorts—a xenophobia that has hamstrung the very regionalism that reflective Africans concede to be essential for their advancement. "To quote an old Scottish saying," one conspicuously non-Gaelic Nigerian foreign-office functionary told me, "'You can do without your friends but not without your neighbors.'" There has always been an undercurrent of suspiciousness about foreigners in Africa; after independence, many Congolese were resentful of all outsiders, among whom they lumped other Congolese who had been abroad. (Following the eruptions of the 1960s that plagued the Congo, fifty thousand Congolese crossed their eastern border and took refuge in Uganda; lately the Congo government has been placing ads in Uganda papers, inviting them back.) And there had until recently always been a flow of Africans back and forth across national boundaries. Unemployed Hausas from Chad, who were indistinguishable from Hausas in Nigeria, would drift south across their common border and join the Nigerian army; the Luos in Kenya and the Luos in Uganda would wander back and forth across their common border in search of jobs or family companionship; one talks to a group of inmates of a Dakar prison and finds that a remarkably large number of them are aliens: Here is a man wearing a Lenin pin (how many prisons elsewhere would permit it?) who says he is not a Communist but merely a student from Mali who has already served four years for hurting a *flic* in a fight; there is a man who

45

says he is a Catholic from Togo who got a Senegalese Muslim girl pregnant and, when he asked to marry her, was instead turned over by her parents to the police.

In the francophone countries of West Africa, free-and-easy migration used to be commonplace. Even now, some five hundred thousand of Guinea's three million indigenes live elsewhere, and half the population of Abidjan consists of non-Ivorians. At any given time, there are probably half a million Upper Voltans living in the Ivory Coast; Upper Volta is poor, and few Ivorians fancy the menial jobs—crop-picking, night-soil-collecting, and the like— that Upper Voltans are glad to fill. The Ivory Coast has granted certain voting rights to African expatriates, and its émigrés from Upper Volta, Guinea, and Mali have been elected to its National Assembly; but the only time Houphouët-Boigny was ever balked by the Assembly was when, in 1967, he proposed dual citizenship for his resident *Voltaiques*. In the colonial era, the British, too, condoned migration; many Nigerians drifted into the Gold Coast, now Ghana; and Ghanaians, for their part, ranged the Guinea coast; they and the Senegalese are the only littoral people who care about fishing, and most of the thatched fishermen's shacks one sees along the shores of Togo and Dahomey are Ghanaians' homes.

But now things are changing across the continent. The welcome wagon has stalled. Ivorians are claiming that ninety-five percent of the crimes in their country are committed by foreigners. Tanzanians blame Kenyans for *their* crime. Ugandans have been deporting Kenyans (to the detriment of the service at Kampala's main hotel, where the best waiters were Kenyan Luos), and Uganda and Kenya have been squabbling over the allegiance of the gifted legs of a middle-distance runner who represented Uganda in the 1970 Commonwealth Games at Edinburgh, when, ostensibly a Ugandan, he was a warden in the Ugandan prison system; now he is in the Kenyan prison system, says he was really a Kenyan all along, and wants to run in Kenyan colors. I met one black man in Nairobi, working for the Kenyan government, who said he had Africanized an Englishman out of a job in Kampala a couple of years back; then he had been Ugandanized out of the job himself. Sierra Leone has been expelling Ghanaians once made to feel at home, and Ghana's long-time hospitality to Nigerians and others, but especially to Nigerians, ended abruptly at the end of 1969 with the passage by the Accra government of an Alien Expulsion Act. Some ten thousand Nigerians were summarily escorted to Ghana's eastern border.

Meanwhile, Ghana was accusing Togo of responsibility for its increase in child-stealing, and the Togolese, joining the swelling African chorus, were accusing Ghanaians of all sorts of peccadilloes. The Ivory Coast blamed a visiting soccer team from Guinea for its recent outbreak of cholera, and when the epidemic reached Ghana, Ghana blamed it on Togo, which was easier than calling attention to the utter lack of a public sewage-disposal system in Accra. Specifically, Ghana charged that some Togolese smugglers had dumped the body of a cholera victim on Ghana soil rather than dispose of it on their own.

Smuggling is a major industry in a number of small African countries that have no other ready access to foreign exchange. The British ambassador to Togo not long ago received a query from his puzzled home office: How could he account for the fact that Scotch exports to Togo, a not notoriously whiskey-drinking nation, had doubled in a year? Dahomey grows no cocoa, but its neighbor Nigeria does, and eight thousand tons of cocoa were exported from Dahomey in 1970. The cholera epidemic was not only a threat to Togo's health but to its economy, inasmuch as when the disease hit that country its government felt obliged to put a couple of key smuggling communities in trade-stifling quarantine.

That the francophone Africans and the anglophone Africans have generally mingled, when they mingled at all, in accordance with colonial practices is attributable not only to shared languages (despite the concern of American blacks for Swahili as an African lingua franca, that language is hardly spoken west of the Congo; West Africa has two linguae francae—English and French), but to the patterns of communication and transportation established in colonial days. African colonies often kept in touch with one another not bilaterally but through England or France, or, in the case of the Congo, through Belgium. Even today, Iberian Airlines billboards in Kinshasa urge travelers to stop off at Madrid—en route to Brussels.

A singular anomaly among the new nations is Cameroon, which

47

is part anglophone, part francophone (some call it "franglophone"), and teaches both English and French in its schools. True, the French-speaking presidents of both Niger and Dahomey have lately been taking English lessons, but they have special economic motivation: Both their countries abut, and would like to be financially abetted by, anglophone Nigeria. President Houphouët-Boigny, whose economy is running so smoothly he does not have to polish his English, believes that linguistic differences pose no threat to African development—only ideological differences. "I have dear friends among the anglophones," he says. "There is no reason we can't eventually have an Africa that, like Canada, is divided only by languages. The real danger we face is from Marxist ideas."

The francophone countries tend to be more dependent on, and devoted to, their former rulers than do the anglophone. Britain's ex-colonies—particularly Tanzania, Uganda, and Nigeria—complained heatedly about the possibility of Britain's selling arms to South Africa; France's ex-colonies barely murmured about the actuality of France's selling them. A British Prime Minister would find it uncomfortable to visit much of anglophone Africa today; President Pompidou was widely acclaimed when he visited five francophone countries early in 1971. He brightened the atmosphere just before turning up by announcing that France was increasing its already formidable aid to Africa by fifteen percent, bringing it to two hundred million dollars a year. France helps francophone Africa, furthermore, with considerable manpower—ten thousand coöperants annually, who elect to serve two years on the continent in lieu of military service, and whose salaries are paid by France. And many Frenchmen still live permanently in Senegal, the Ivory Coast, Gabon, and the others.

For a number of French who spent long years in government service in Indochina and married Asians, France was too chilly for their families, so they settled in Africa. A number of them with Indochinese wives opened small businesses. There are thirty Vietnamese restaurants in Abidjan alone; one of these, the Mekong, is located next door to the United States Information Service. ("I suppose if they get into trouble we'll have to bail them out," an American foreign service officer told me.) Senegalese have a peculiar attachment to poor-quality rice. In the old days, the French would shuttle rice ships between Saigon and Paris; the substandard cargo was dumped off at Dakar, and it became part of the Senegalese diet. When at three o'clock one morning I flew into Dakar, my first African port of entry, thirsting for authentic local sights and sounds, it was strange to come upon several dozen young French residents of Senegal heading toward France for *their* military service and, at that grim hour, milling about the air terminal singing, with French lyrics, *Auld Lang Syne*.

The present rulers of francophone Africa are a quasi-French French-educated elite. Every Dahomeyan of consequence has spent his seven years in France, and the educated upper classes of that country speak French at home. At Abomey, historical seat of the bloodthirsty Dahomeyan kings who swapped slaves for guns and who rested their thrones on the skulls of decapitated enemies, one sees stores called "Chic-Chic," "Joli-Joli," and "Aux Elegants." The French ambassador to Senegal is automatically the doyen of the diplomatic corps there, length of service notwithstanding. President Senghor of Senegal has a farm in Normandy, where he goes every August, the traditional holiday month for France; in Dakar, it is difficult to see him without going through a French intermediary. Bottled water is flown into Dakar from Paris, and the bulk of the profits from the French-owned retail stores there, being freely convertible into French francs, are flown out. When I complained to a Senegalese waiter at a Dakar sidewalk café about an outrageous overcharge, he shrugged and replied what could you expect, the proprietor was French. Grateful for the African's sympathy, I overtipped on the surcharge.

At the University of Abidjan, eighty percent of the faculty is French. There is an Institute of African History on the campus, but its director, one of the few Ivorian professors around, has hardly any equipment in his office except—how French!—four rubber stamps. After a lecture there by another African, on local attitudes toward colonialism, a student asked a question about President Houphouët-Boigny and *his* attitudes. "But he's not an African," the lecturer said, "he's a *Frenchman*." Houphouët-Boigny, who spent much of his adult life in Paris, serving in the French National Assembly from 1946 to 1959, still also vacations on the continent. His principal advisor, a West Indian from Martinique, is reliably said to have a French passport. (If in Abidjan one needs a visa for Dahomey or Cameroon, one gets it from the French Embassy.) When Prime Minister Busia of anglophone Ghana made a state visit to the Ivory Coast, the official interpreter was a white Frenchman. The Secretary of the Abidjan Junior Chamber of Commerce is French, and at a recent lunch of the American Business Club there, while the only flags on display were those of the United States and the Ivory Coast, all the speeches were in French.

In most former African colonies, there are fewer expatriates around now than there were at independence time. The Ivory Coast had eighteen thousand resident Frenchmen when it achieved sovereignty. Now it has thirty-five thousand. The French still have a tennis club in Abidjan to which not only are no Ivorians admitted but no non-French whites, either. The most popular discotheque in Abidjan, a city many of whose residents regard *Le Monde* as their hometown paper, is a decommissioned French submarine, moored at a lagoon dock. The reason the French remain so prominent in the Ivory Coast is simple. Houphouët-Boigny's primary concern is economic, and to achieve prosperity he is convinced he needs all the French help he can get. This situation is eminently satisfactory to the French. For one thing, without a continuing presence in the francophone states of Africa, France would have little pretext for regarding itself, in world councils, as a superpower. For another, its own prosperity is involved. As from Senegal, profits return to France from the Ivory Coast— probably fifty million dollars' worth annually from this country alone.

Whereas the French colonialists, with a policy of direct rule, trained Africans to be black Frenchmen, the British, with a policy of indirect rule, trained them to be African administrators. "The French hang around francophone Africa sort of pretending not to be there but so visible you'd have to be blind to ignore them," a Nigerian told me. "On the other hand, at independence time, the British said to their former wards, 'O.K., you've grown up now, go out into the world on your own, and if you ever get really stuck, remember that we're always good for a fiver.'" Some Africans now believe that perhaps both colonial powers missed the boat. "The British made Africans bureaucrats, and the French made them philosophers," a Kenyan said, "but nobody taught them how to work with their hands."

The legacies the two countries left behind are quite different, and quite characteristic of the respective donors. For Western palates, the food is much better in francophone Africa. European housewives from anglophone Ghana often drive two hours to Lomé, in francophone Togo, to stock up on good French cheese, wine, fruit, and bread. The British left Brussels sprouts behind them, and a typical restaurant menu in anglophone Africa is apt to feature steak-and-kidney-pie and trifle. The British left a lot more, too; a decade after their cessation of authority, their influence is still astoundingly noticeable. Moving around Africa from country to country, one can easily get confused about many things, but there can never be much doubt whether one is in an anglophone or a francophone nation; the anglophone nations are those in which the ritual of morning tea is still faithfully observed.

And in which polo is still enthusiastically played. The Lagos Polo Club recently completed an extension to its facilities, and in northern Nigeria, up at Kaduna, the American Consul General, assigned there not long after being on the polo team at Yale, was delighted to find that he could indulge in his favorite recreation three times a week. (Northern Nigeria used to be the prestigious station for British foreign service types posted to West Africa; the story goes that after a boatload of them left London, those who debarked first, at Bathurst, in The Gambia, were scorned; those dropped next at Freetown, in Sierra Leone, were pitied; those who got as far as Accra were considered not quite so bad off; those who made it to Lagos in southern Nigeria were considered to be tolerably well placed; but those sent to Kaduna—ah, they were the chaps with the ruddy good luck!) The Emir of Katsuna, in northern Nigeria, the father of the Nigerian army chief of staff, is that country's only six-goal polo player; the secretary of Ghana's national polo organization is the army chief of staff himself. Telephone an Englishman's home in Accra on a weekend and you are likely to hear his houseman say, "He's gone to polo, please." There still are golf courses in the middle of Nairobi and Kampala, and in

Ibadan, the capital of Western Nigeria, when the indigenous commissioner of police learned that the ranking British diplomat in town was a golf nut, he took up the game himself to help fill out the foreigner's weekly foursome.

And so it goes throughout anglophone Africa these days. A Sunday visit to a racetrack on the outskirts of Nairobi makes one think one has somehow been whisked to Ascot or Epsom Downs —shooting sticks, Labrador retrievers, nannies with scrubbed white children, even, the temperature notwithstanding, Colonel Blimps in scratchy tweeds. A few miles off, in the chaste paneled chambers of the Muthaiga Country Club, where the man at the next table may well be the Duke of Manchester, the white up-country landholders still convene, as if there had never been a Mau Mau, and sip their pink gins. Nairobi itself boasts the only stage repertory company in East Africa; it is almost too much to believe, but it is true, that their offering next week is *East Lynne*.

Relatively few Africans, of course, play polo or go to the races— most Africans live in the bush, miles from any foreign influences, or local ones, either—but in the anglophone countries English habits are rife. Not until several years after the civil service in Uganda was Ugandanized did the government abolish the inherited custom of providing its civil servants with regular home leave—to England. At one dinner honoring the tenth anniversary of Ugandan independence, there were no Englishmen in attendance, but the toastmaster nonetheless got the post-prandial proceedings under way with "Milords and miladies, pray silence and charge your glasses." In the anglophone countries, traffic still drives to the left, and East African Airways planes carry the *London Illustrated News*. As Paris is the Mecca for many francophone Africans, so is London for the anglophones. A Lagos salon proclaims that it has a "London-trained hairdresser and beautician," a Kaduna day nursery-school a "London-trained proprietress." So enamored are many Africans of the British way of life that outside a hole-in-the-wall emporium in the public market of Ibadan one sees the sign, "Office of the Managing Director," and a Ghanaian school has a Mfantsipim Old Boys Association.

At the same time that most of East Africa, early in 1971, was thundering against Prime Minister Heath about arms for South

Africa, Kenyans were turning out in colonial-size droves to welcome the Prince of Wales. Of course, he was an authority figure,
if only a presumptive one, but he was also royalty, and Africans
are fond of royalty, foreign and domestic. As in London the appearance of the Queen Mother may make or break the opening of
a foundling home, so in Accra is the appearance of the Queen
Mother of Akwapim the high point of an inauguration ceremony
of a society of Akropong citizens. And how some Ghanaians seem
to venerate their former despots! At one diplomatic function, the
British High Commissioner told some rather feeble jokes. The
Ghanaians within earshot, a highly placed and highly intelligent
representation of their countrymen, fell all over themselves in
hysterical laughter; it was as if they'd been permanently brainwashed—as, of course, maybe they had. One Ghanaian tribe even
has a white British chief, a former district commissioner still contentedly in residence. Ghanaian chiefs have stools as their symbols
of power—the land over which they preside is called stool land,
and the Coming Down of the Golden Stool is a holy event in the
Ashanti religion—and once a year, following their long-standing
tradition, the disciples of the white British chief enstool him on
a palanquin and carry him around on their heads. It is no simple
matter, for this particular black man's burden weighs three hundred pounds.

The British veneer is beginning to crack. Zambia, for instance,
has lately done away with wigs and gowns in its courts. If Africans
are conscious of their similarities to their old masters, they are also
conscious of their differences. The old street names are disappear-
ing, the King George VI and Balfour Avenues becoming Lumumba or Luthuli. In Nairobi, the same pedestal that used to support a statue of Queen Elizabeth and her crown now supports
one of Mzee Kenyatta and his fly whisk. And when the President
of Uganda was asked last year by a BBC interviewer if he spoke
the same kind of English as other Commonwealth people, he replied, "No, I do not speak the same English as you do. I am not
English. I paid money to learn English. You did not pay money
to learn English."

4

It was at a Berlin conference in 1883 that the colonial masters of most of Africa established the boundaries that are still largely observed by the continent's independent black nations. The borders were prescribed with little regard for geography or ethnography; in independent Africa today, there are a dozen rivers that pass through two or more countries. The result was a hodge-podge of dispersed groups with little evident rationale for being placed together—or, even more importantly, perhaps, for being set apart. Established tribes found themselves half in one new political entity, half in another. Dahomeyans, in the current wave of xenophobia, often say that the wily Togolese do them in at every turn; when reminded that they are castigating, among others, their blood brothers, who just happen to be separated from them by an arbitrary, artificial dividing line, they change the subject. (Family ties across a border, however, can be helpful to smugglers.)

Yet with a few minor exceptions most of the emerging countries have been surprisingly unargumentative about the borders they inherited. When the Organization of African Unity started up in 1963, one of the few issues all hands could agree on was that the old boundaries, no matter how unfair (Liberia, for instance, has long asserted that the French welshed on a promise to return to it part of what is now Guinea), would be held inviolable. And after a decade of living within these boundaries, they have achieved a certain *de facto* legitimacy. Anyway, if one of them were altered, another might have to be, and a game of falling dominoes could ensue wilder than any ever contemplated for Asia.

Still, as a result of the Berlin conference, the map of Africa took on a strange appearance. The former British colony of The Gambia (the "The" derives from its consisting mainly of the banks of the Gambia River) is almost completely swallowed up by the former French colony of Senegal. Throughout their independence, these two particular countries have been negotiating fitfully to establish an acceptable modus vivendi—never an easy thing when one country fancies cricket and another bicycle-riding —but while accord has been reached on quite a few minor matters, such as hydrological and ichthyological studies, there still has been no meeting of minds on the one big matter of mutual concern: tariffs. The Gambia, whose main industry is smuggling (it is said to have more transistor radios per capita than any nation on earth), can legally import cement more cheaply from England than from Senegal.

Several distant countries, among them the United States, which has steadily maintained a tight-purse attitude toward Africa, use the same ambassador for Senegal and The Gambia. Small The Gambia has an air of informality that larger Senegal lacks. When the American ambassador made the routine presentation of some lunar-rock fragments to the Gambian president, along with a Gambian flag that had been to the moon, the head of the state asked his chief of protocol where his photographer was, and when the chief of protocol said, "He forgot his camera," the president said, "Never mind, I'll run upstairs and get mine."

Both Senegal and The Gambia grow peanuts. Gambian farmers get cash for theirs. Senegalese farmers get government IOUs, and they have to sign five-year government production contracts that most of them can't read, and they complain that the government overcharges them for fertilizer. Moreover, the peanut market has lately been depressed. The latest crop was the smallest in sixteen years. It was the rule of thumb ten years ago, furthermore, that for every bag of peanuts Senegal exported it could import a bag of rice. Now it's three bags of peanuts for one of rice.

Peanuts aside—and once one dismisses peanuts there is not much left to the Senegalese economy—Senegal's chief attribute is Dakar, a very French city of six hundred thousand struggling to sustain its reputation as the Paris of Africa. One can still enter a restaurant in the heart of Dakar and encounter not a single black customer. Until 1904, the French colonial headquarters in Senegal were at the inland city of St. Louis, otherwise noted chiefly for the obesity of its indigenous women, whose attractiveness was measured by their avoirdupois; the most hugely esteemed among them had to be carried around in pony carts. When France made Dakar its colonial capital, it was envisioned as the hub of francophone Africa, and it was made the repository of a good many fancy government structures, which today are obsolete.

Still, Dakar remains the gateway to West Africa, and when the Suez Canal was closed its residents anticipated a sharp increase in the use of their port facilities. But they dashed their own hopes by raising harbor taxes so high that most ships steamed by without even a passing toot. Dakar was left with little more than an overblown bureaucracy. Of the forty-five thousand individuals in the city who are salaried, nearly half are civil servants, and this proliferation of functionaries, another hand-me-down from the French, imposes a heavy burden on the nation.

Senegal is a troubled country, and a nervous one. During the November, 1970, invasion of next-door Guinea, an aircraft carrier was spotted off Dakar, not far from Gorée Island, the African obverse of Ellis Island. Near the Rue des Dongeons there is a seventeenth-century Dutch fort that once held slaves and now is a Senegalese prison. The inmates freely roam the island in the daytime, sprucing it up for visitors—not a few of whom are from the United States and want to set foot on the spot where, as some put it, black America began. The news that the aircraft carrier was in the vicinity sparked a flurry of rumors in Dakar. Of what ominous nationality could it be? Portuguese? United States? Soviet? French, preferably? When the ship got closer, it proved to be a surplus Canadian vessel that had been sold to the Republic of China and was being towed to Taiwan by a Japanese tugboat. Dakar calmed down, and the prisoners at Gorée, who may have entertained fleeting hopes of deliverance, went back to sweeping its historic streets.

At the death of Charles de Gaulle, few more effusive testimonials were paid to him than those of the francophone nations who revered him as the Decolonizer of Africa. The Ivory Coast observed eight days of mourning. Even the government of Guinea, which had less reason than most to acclaim the General, issued a statement characterizing him as a great leader of French independence, though it was careful to say nothing about African independence. The reason was that when in 1958 de Gaulle told his African dependencies to answer "*Oui*" or "*Non*" to the question of joining a French African community in the brief interim period before complete independence, every colony said "*Oui*" except Guinea. De Gaulle's reaction had been swift and stern: France pulled its technicians out of Guinea, pulled out its financial backing, even pulled out its plumbing fixtures. (Guinea is conspicuously absent from the multinational francophone West African telephone directory; France had also pulled out its phones.) Ever since, just about the only visible asset of Guinea—aside from a fierce chauvinistic pride—has been its peripatetic Ballets Africains. Touring the United States in 1959, they created a mild furor when they tried vainly to perform in their routine bare-breasted fashion at a midtown New York theatre. (In the winter of 1971, they performed topless in Harlem, without raising an eyebrow.) Africans, having long taken the human body in stride, are understandably cynical about shifting Western attitudes toward nudity. While some Africans are not above exploiting their own customs for prurient white foreigners—along Tanzanian roads, tourists' cars are halted by young girls, hopping up and down, bare breasts bobbing, who offer to do a dance for a shilling apiece—others think foreigners behave very strangely. "One trouble with you Americans," a Guinean I met in Abidjan told me, "is that you really can't bring yourselves to believe that not all Africans go around naked shouting '*Bwana!*' You have this terrible double standard. First you make our ballet girls put on bras, and then you

58

come along with *Hair* and *Oh! Calcutta!*, which I personally thought displayed a very unhealthy attitude toward sex. When I myself was studying in New York, there was a party for us Africans at International House, and it was suggested we all wear native dress. So I got out my *kente* cloth, and some smirking American lady came up and asked me if I wore pants underneath. And then some other African man did an African dance, all by himself, and another American asked me if he was supposed to be fighting, and I said, 'What a silly question! Have you ever seen anybody fight alone?' "

Guinea's long-range economic prospects are sanguine. The country has large untapped quantities of copper, tin, lead, and zinc, and it has twenty-five percent of the earth's known reserves of high-grade bauxite, the ore that produces aluminum. The bauxite is currently being developed by Guinea with the assistance of a consortium of French, Canadian, and American industrialists, who, being hard-headed businessmen, are unconcerned both with Sekou Touré's somewhat heavy-handed approach to justice (he hangs people publicly) and with his leftist ideology. His best foreign friends come from Peking. One of the few Americans, aside from businessmen and diplomats, who was admitted to Guinea between 1969 and 1971 accompanied President Touré, who liked to drive himself around Conakry, without bodyguards, in a Citroen, to a People's Congress Hall built with Chinese funds. Inside, looming over the stage, was the largest portrait of Mao Tse-Tung the visitor had ever seen. *"Mon cher Président, ou est* votre *photo?"* the American inquired. The next day Mao's picture came down, and one of Touré went up.

President Touré and President Houphouët-Boigny were both charter members, a quarter of a century ago, of the Rassemblement Democratique Africain, a group in the van of the independence movement in francophone Africa. The two men have moved far apart. Touré periodically accuses Houphouët-Boigny of plotting his death, and their countries have no diplomatic relations. This is not to say that the two veteran leaders may not pick up again where they left off. Touré, especially, has a way of switching friendships. He was awarded the Lenin Peace Prize one year and threw out the Russian diplomats accredited to him the next; *they* were plotting his demise, he said. Houphouët-Boigny has been more consistent. He has had no relations with any Communist nation, and his "*Oui*" to De Gaulle was so loud that its echoes still reverberate. He has been unapologetic about the French presence in his land. He is willing to sacrifice a degree of political independence to establish a solid basis for economic growth. As one Ivorian close to him put it, "It's better to have a small slice of a big pie than a big slice of a little one." It may take the Ivory Coast a quarter of a century or more, with the French holding the pie knife, to achieve true economic self-sufficiency; whether this policy will ultimately put the Ivory Coast twenty-five years ahead of Guinea or twenty-five years behind is moot.

In any event, the French grip on Ivorian life is firm. In the Ivory Coast's secondary schools today, there are fewer than three hundred Ivorian teachers and nearly two thousand French. Other nations have moved into the economy of the Ivory Coast, whose stability they admire—the Japanese with their textiles, West Germans in pineapple cultivation, Dutch in wax-print-making, Americans in dry-cell batteries—but the French still provide the bulk of the advisers, technicians, and businessmen. "This country has a rich potential," Houphouët-Boigny says, "but at present we lack a cadre of Ivorians to realize it. So I must address myself to the white world for assistance." Whether economic development is necessarily a precursor of social development is also moot, but for the time being the Ivory Coast is showing the way to its francophone neighbors; in 1970 its operating and investment budgets came to thirty-five million dollars more than the combined budgets of Senegal, Gabon, and Cameroon, which among them have twice its population.

Because the economic picture is so relatively rosy in the Ivory Coast, it suffers less than most other emerging African countries from brain drain. Students from other nations who go abroad to learn skills often don't bother to come back. Ivorians do; they want to get rich, and the aura of prosperity in which Abidjan basks lures them home. The capital city is not, as some of Houphouët-Boigny's critics have charged, merely a copy of a French metropolis. It has a distinctive African flavor: hand laundry done in the lagoon and spread to dry at the edge of the city's broad avenues; a barber shop, in the center of town, consisting simply of an African *barbier* and an African customer, sitting on the ground face to face, the one shaving the other with a straight razor. And there is nothing European about the sprawling, two-story market in the African quarter of Treichville, where hardly a word of French is heard, where upstairs yard goods can be converted into dresses on the spot by hundreds of African women perched behind sewing machines, and where downstairs the choosy consumer can finger a wide range of live turkeys and pigeons or dried lizards and cats' heads. In Abidjan, space is at a premium. A thousand acres of land were reclaimed from its lagoon, in 1970, and every square inch was at once grabbed up for new factories; mere word that an additional two hundred and fifty acres would be created produced a waiting list of prospective occupants.

Across the Abidjan lagoon from the center of the city stands what may prove to be Houphouët-Boigny's grandest monument— the Hotel Ivoire, an edifice so dazzling and complex it perhaps deserves less to be compared to another hotel than to a Japanese department store. Begun in 1963 (a new wing was added in 1970), and fifty-percent-owned by the government, the Ivoire, along with the conventional hotel amenities, boasts a movie theatre, a supermarket, bowling alleys, the largest art emporium in West Africa, if not all Africa, and the only ice-skating rink on the continent. Ivorian teenagers go there in droves after school, and skates are selling like cats' heads in Abidjan shoe stores. The big hotel also has a gambling casino, from which Ivorians of all ages are barred; Houphouët-Boigny doesn't want them squandering their wages on roulette or baccarat. He did, not long ago, permit the inauguration of a national lottery, principally because Ivorians had been patronizing lotteries in Togo, Dahomey, and Upper Volta.

The Hotel Ivoire is usually crowded, but few adult Ivorians frequent it. One Ivorian businessman told me he felt less at home there than in Paris, New York, or Tokyo. The inspiration for the hotel came shortly after the Ivory Coast became independent, when Houphouët-Boigny visited Liberia. He stayed at the then new and impressive Ducor Intercontinental Hotel in Monrovia, and asked to be put in touch with the chap who had constructed it. That was a far-ranging entrepreneur named Moshe Mayer, a Pole

61

from Rumania whose family migrated to Palestine in the 1920s. Mayer prospered in construction there (he built the thirty-story Shalom Tower in Tel Aviv), branched out into textiles, and ended up as the principal partner in a Geneva-based organization with diverse interests called the Mafit Trust, which now owns the other half of the Ivoire.

The Abidjan hotel has lately had on display scale models and drawings for an even more ambitious joint project, a two-billion-dollar undertaking to be called the African Riviera. It is scheduled for completion, if all goes according to plan, in 1981. Covering ten thousand acres, it will incorporate several new hotels, an international convention center, residential communities for a hundred and twenty thousand people, an African counterpart of Disneyland, and a game reserve on a man-made island—the animals to be viewed in safety and comfort from monorails passing at least high enough to clear giraffes.

The Riviera will be situated near the Ivoire on the outskirts of Cocody, the fancy residential section of Abidjan, where most cabinet ministers and diplomats have their homes. Houphouët-Boigny lives there himself—next door, appropriately, to the French ambassador. Over the living-room couch on which the president sits while receiving visitors, equally appropriately, is a Chagall landscape of Nice. Houphouët-Boigny, who was born in 1905, has an ideally balanced background for a contemporary African leader; he is a Catholic with a couple of authentic witch doctors among his ancestors, and in his youth he specialized in both medicine and agriculture. He was also the first West African to serve as a French cabinet minister. Short-haired, round-faced, and the epitome of Gallic suaveness, he likes to keep himself au courant by arranging conversations with constituents from all walks of Ivorian life—tribal chiefs, government functionaries, market women, witch doctors, and university professors. Houphouët-Boigny calls these informative sessions "dialogues," and values them highly. When, following a demonstration at the University of Abidjan, the students involved declined to engage in colloquy with him, he was so offended that he had five hundred foreigners among them roused from their dormitory beds at six one morning and packed off to Togo, Mali, Niger, Dahomey, and Upper Volta.

Most recently, Houphouët-Boigny emerged as black Africa's most outspoken advocate of a much touchier kind of dialogue—one with the Republic of South Africa. For an African politician to take such a stance—even one who gets ninety-nine per cent of the vote—was ticklish business (though it became less ticklish after President Nixon announced he was going to Peking), but the Ivorian president is an economy-minded man, and South Africa is far and away the most prosperous and most industrialized nation on the continent. Besides, if Houphouët-Boigny could engage in fruitful dialogue with Lebanese merchants and coffee growers, why not with John Vorster? Merely to talk to someone, the Ivorian leader argued, did not imply condoning all his practices, and in any event there had to be some way other than violence to solve the prickly problem of South Africa's relations with the rest of the continent. Houphouët-Boigny believed that other Africans had been unrealistic and self-destructive in their unbending attitudes toward South Africa; to seek to overthrow its government by force might, he was convinced, invite the Communists to move in on Africa in force themselves, and in his view Communism was worse than apartheid.

The reactions of many other Africans to the feelers Houphouët-Boigny put out were predictable and peppery. He got a sympathetic hearing in countries like Malawi, Mauritius, and Lesotho, but these were small nations very much in the South African orbit; the president of Malawi, Dr. H. Kamuzu Banda, was the first black African head of state of go to South Africa and thus publicly reveal himself to have an active case of what some South Africans have called "dialogitis." The Ivorian found an ally closer at hand in the person of Prime Minister Kofi Busia of Ghana, who observed that there was no reason why nations couldn't simultaneously talk and fight—look at Korea, look at Vietnam—and that anyway when it came to supporting African freedom fighters, only six of forty-one nations pledged to support the Liberation Committee of the OAU (Ghana among the six) were fully paid up in their assessments. (Ghana's foreign minister declared at an Organization of African Unity meeting at Addis Ababa in June, 1971, that in view of all the delinquencies, "OAU" seemed a less fitting abbreviation for the group than "IOU.") Dialogue, Busia insisted, was "but another weapon in the armoury of the strategy for the elimination of apartheid and

the erection of a multiracial society in South Africa." For Busia
to declare himself also took gumption, since white southern Africans are very much *bêtes noirs* in Ghana: there, as in several other
black African countries, prospective visitors are generally denied
admittance, let alone conversation, if they have a South African or
Rhodesian passport.

Most African leaders, however, were quick to dissociate themselves from Houphouët-Boigny's position. Radio South Africa,
which admired the position, declared that President Kaunda of
Zambia "was left speechless," but he wasn't; he suggested—and
other African leaders like General Gowon of Nigeria soon echoed
his words—that if white South Africans wanted a dialogue with
any black Africans they should hold one with their own black
Africans. Privately, Kaunda, who lives just north of Rhodesia and
has vital economic links with the countries to his south, would
have liked to explore the possibility of talks with South Africa,
but he wasn't able to figure out a way of endorsing the notion
without giving the South Africans a chance to take advantage of
any move he might make and thus gain a mite of respectability
for a regime that to him is anathema. So, publicly, he denounced
the idea and said things like "The concept of dialogue sounds as
French as the nonaggression pact proposed by South Africa sounds
British." (In his capital city of Lusaka, the *Daily Mail* went a step
further and called Houphouët-Boigny "the most detestable quis-
ling of our time.") Some African leaders, following a similar tack,
went so far as to hint that Houphouët-Boigny and Busia had
actually been bribed by the French to take their conciliatory stand.
As one high Zambian official put it to me, "All we know is that
these men keep going to France, and there must be something
going on there that gives them their ideas." Whether the rumor
was true or not was probably unimportant; in Africa, people often
react not so much to what has happened as to what is believed.

In the winter of 1971, Houphouët-Boigny even thought of holding an exploratory get-together with some white South Africans
in Abidjan, strictly to discuss economic give-and-take. After all, he
reasoned, many black African countries, whatever their political
stance, traded with South Africa; the Congolese army used South
African provisions. The Ivorian president backed off, though, and

had to content himself for the time being with an off-the-record meeting in Paris between some of his people and some South Africans; a few months after that, an "unofficial" delegation of middle-level Ivorians actually visited South Africa. Houphouët-Boigny was saddened, but not discouraged, by all the brouhaha his proposal stirred up. "I expected the reaction I got," he told me. "The problem of South Africa has touched the nerves of all blacks. But I have a right to say what I think. We're all against the racial situation in South Africa, and yet is not South Africa an African country? Our brothers there are not asking the white South Africans to get out. They're asking only for racial equality, and for living in peace. You can attain peace by negotiation or by force. We're familiar with the peace of the colonials; that's peace by force. But is that desirable? Force is not a solution. And to say we're going to come in by force to save the black South Africans is a fantasy. So you have to keep looking for the dialogue."

5

Africans have learned a lot from the West. They have learned to hedge their bets. Thus while the official position of Ivory Coast's neighbor Liberia has been that a dialogue with South Africa is unthinkable, one government official there told me, guardedly, that he hoped no one "would dismiss the possibility that there might be some merit in it." Liberia has two basic groups—its so-called Americo-Liberians, who are descended from the freed slaves who originally settled it; and its so-called aborigines, who constitute everybody else. Of Liberia's one million, two hundred thousand residents, fewer than five percent are Americo-Liberians, but they have traditionally been the ruling class. Nowadays, they are somewhat embarrassed about their slave origins (though they themselves condoned some local slavery well into the twentieth century); when an American sociologist doing research on slavery told a Liberian woman that he had come upon an old ship's manifest listing a grandfather of hers as part of its human cargo, instead of being proud of or even interested in this new-found intelligence about her heritage, she begged him not to tell anybody else.

Liberia is an odd country, oddly situated. In an area of West

Africa where every other country is either anglophone or francophone, it is neither. (President Tubman once remarked wryly that the trouble with Liberia was that it had enjoyed none of the benefits of colonialism.) Nor can it truly be said to be "americanophone." Because there are so relatively few Americo-Liberians and because in any event many of the original freed slaves were uneducated, the English that is the lingua franca of Liberia is hard for an American to comprehend—harder, even, than the similarly singsong dialect of the West Indies. I spent several hours one day crossing a lake to visit a seemingly beguiling spot that I understood from a guide harbored some "cave men"; on arrival, I discovered that he was referring to the name of the place—Cape Mount.

There are superficial resemblances in Liberia to the United States: a flag with stripes and one star (symbolizing the first independent black nation of Africa), American-style mailboxes, counties called Maryland, Virginia, and Kentucky; and American paper money as the national currency. (American and Liberian coins are used interchangeably.) But the ties between Liberia and its parent country are gossamer. Liberia became a nation in 1847, and has had precious little help from the United States ever since. America was glad to get rid of the freed slaves who founded Liberia; once out of sight, they were pretty much out of mind. The United States ignored brutal British raids across Liberia's borders in the mid-nineteenth century; Washington was hoping that London would side with the North in the impending Civil War. Not until 1862, after the war had begun, did the United States even formally recognize Liberia. And there has been little practical assistance ever since, except when it suited American foreign or military policy to tender it.

But some of American history has been intertwined with Liberian history. Up the Mesurado River from Monrovia, the coastal capital, lies Clayashland, a town revered by Liberians because it was there that its single political party, the True Whig Party, was launched. At Clayashland, named after Henry Clay and his old Kentucky home, there are ruins of spacious, bay-windowed houses that seem straight out of the antebellum American south. Old-fashioned Liberians, like some old-fashioned black Americans, are partial to elaborate funerals and elaborate gravestones. In a cemetery at Clayashland, there is a six-foot-high tombstone containing an astonishingly detailed biography of a lady church worker and educator, born in Louisiana; among the curriculum vitae chiseled into the monument is the fact that she once met Mrs. Franklin D. Roosevelt. Many Liberians, too, have names that sound like very elegant American social-register names, and these are apt to be displayed, in full, on driveway signs outside their bearers' homes. Liberians, moreover, are partial to a high-toned, naked, introductory initial; prominent in Liberia's ruling circle are, among others, E. Jonathan Goodridge, T. Ernest Eastman, J. Rudolph Grimes, and S. Harding Smythe. Nonetheless, how strikingly different Liberians are from Americans was borne home to me one day when the driver of a taxi I was riding in bawled out another driver for cutting in front of him, and then apologized over his shoulder for using the word "hell."

Liberia is a pious, fundamentalist country, at least on Sunday. The rest of the time, it swings. It is the one African country that has a fair number of Uncle Tom stereotypes, and in which a visiting American Negro doctor who says the use of the word "black" irritates him can feel really comfortable; some Liberians still use "colored." I met one lacquered-haired American Negro woman there who told me she was enjoying the country hugely and also confided that she was tired of books berating American ghettos; she said ghettos really had a lot of charm. Liberians are partial to formal dress, like middle-class American blacks; they put on men's fashion shows and have a Gentleman-of-the-Year contest. American diplomats put on dark suits and white shirts when they call on Liberian ministers. Liberian men are fascinated by power, pronounced "powah;" power can mean influence or money or sexual virility or all three. (Liberian apothecaries sell powdered power.) Some of the people in government with the most political power can be tough; when one highly placed man bumped into a less potent Liberian's car, he had the innocent party in the crash hauled off to a military stockade and lashed. Primitivism remains widespread in rural Liberia. Ritual murders, complete with liver-eating, still occur in the bush, and as recently as 1935 the losers in a tribal war were flabbergasted, because their witch doctors had assured them they had been rendered bulletproof; they could only conclude that the winners' jujus were stronger than theirs. Not long ago, the chief of staff of the army was imprisoned on a charge of witchcraft.

Until his death in the summer of 1971, President Tubman sought to bridge the long-standing gap between the Americo-Liberians and the Aborigines by bringing more and more of the latter into his government; Liberia has an elitist society, but one can get into it at the bottom and move toward the top. The country's Deputy Minister of Culture never saw a pair of shoes until he was twelve.

In Liberia, whatever Tubman wanted to do was done. He was everybody's irascible, lovable old grandfather, a paramount chief of chiefs with power multiplied to the nth power. When he celebrated his seventy-fifth birthday, in November, 1970, the Ducor International had "Happy Birthday—75" displayed in lights down its entire ten-story façade. Court cases were recessed, and there were so many marathon dinner parties that a few diplomats took to their beds from exhaustion. The legend was that Tubman's presidential palace was equipped with a solid-gold dinner service for a party of a hundred and fifty. Like most Liberian government officials, he had a pleasant farm out in the country; the Tubman place, seventy-two miles from Monrovia, had a private zoo featuring pigmy hippopotamuses, Liberia's chief claim to zoological renown.

A Methodist of conservative bent and, like many highly placed Liberians, an active Mason (the biggest building at Clayashland is a Masonic Lodge, and Monrovia's lodge resembles a huge Greek temple), Tubman, like his neighbor Houphouët-Boigny, avoided formal relations with Communists. But he was a practical politician. He privately entertained the director of the African branch of Moscow's Institute of Politics and the retiring Soviet ambassador to Sierra Leone. The Liberian president also took pains to make himself accessible to his constituents, receiving as many as one hundred of them daily at his palace and jotting down notes of their complaints. "This country very largely depended for a very long time on a very skillful ward politician," one foreign diplomat in Monrovia told me, not without admiration. And for a man held by his people in such awe and veneration, Tubman managed to retain a common touch. He was notable for being able to tell dialect stories without losing his dignity. One of his favorites was a First World War yarn, about the time a German U-boat materialized off Monrovia and began shelling the city. The then president called in a bishop and asked him to invoke divine intercession, and the bishop got down on his knees in prayer and said, "Lawd, come to our aid, and don't send no son because this ain't no child's play." Liberians eat up that sort of thing. Tubman was not president at that time, although some outsiders had the impression he had held that post forever. Actually, he was not elected until 1944.

For many years, Liberia was a one-export country. It granted agreeable concessions to the Firestone rubber company in 1927, and production got under way on a large scale in 1944, when the war cut off the Allies' traditional sources of supply in Asia. Monrovia's international airport is fifty miles from Monrovia, which is inconvenient for most Liberians but is convenient for the nearby Firestone plantation. Now, though, rubber accounts for only fifteen percent of Liberia's exports; iron ore, with seventy-five percent of the total, has moved far into the lead.

The airfield was built by the United States during the Second World War as a military base, at a time when Liberian-American relations were more serene than they are now. In black Africa today, indeed, there is a tendency to regard the United States as not very much interested in the whole continent's problems. There was a flurry of concern during the Kennedy administration, when it was fashionable to acclaim emerging nations, but that has largely subsided; the White House and the State Department don't have time to give Africa high-priority attention, and the Congress has never cared much about it one way or another. During a foreign-aid hearing before the House Committee on Appropriations in March, 1970, a State Department official couldn't remember the name of our ambassador to Nigeria, and the chairman of the committee, Representative Otto E. Passman, referred to Nigeria, the ninth most populous country on earth, as a "little, new emerging nation" that was "still wet behind the ears." When another member of the House arrived in Uganda

71

last year on a Congressional junket, he said to his American Embassy escort, "Tell me, are most of the natives here black?"

Nor do most American businessmen pay much heed to Africa; South Africa excluded, the total American private investment in Africa amounts to a trifling two billion dollars. The fact is that the United States has traditionally regarded Africa as a dependency of Europe, and when we look at Africa we look at it through European eyes. Our detachment notwithstanding, Africans are quite ready to blame United States intervention for anything that goes amiss. There was some reason to believe the British might have been involved in the Ugandan coup of 1971 that saw President Apolo Milton Obote supplanted by General Idi Amin, but little reason to suspect American complicity. Yet when the *Zambia Daily Mail* ran a front-page editorial cartoon on the event, depicting General Amin as a prizefighter in the ring with his hand upraised by a top-hatted figure labelled "Imperialism," the glove on his triumphant fist was further labeled not with a "£" sign but with a "$."

The United States reacts sensitively to charges that it regards Africa as an insignificant continent. "It's important to recognize that it's only recently that we've had an interest in sub-Saharan Africa," says David Newsom, the Assistant Secretary of State for African Affairs. "We have no long-standing commitments to the new nations—none, naturally, dating back before 1957—so it's understandable that in the allocation of the resources we do have Africa rates low. Besides, after independence, the new nations had expectations of help that were probably unrealistic; and also, at a time when there are demands everywhere for our limited aid resources, it should be remembered that Africa gets the largest share of whatever Europe can dole out. But United States credibility is important in black Africa, and we have to try to respond creditably to its growing interest in economic development, trade, and foreign investment." In the last couple of years, nongovernmental Americans in Africa have heard in more than one country —the allegation is not altogether just, but then in Africa it is often the allegation that counts more than the actuality—that there seems to be a tacit quid-pro-quo attached to American largess: that before we promise to deliver any goods, we ask wistfully for just a little support of our policies in Southeast Asia. By and large, though, the American government does not seem overly preoccupied with African feelings. In Abidjan, there was consternation at the disclosure that the code name for the abortive paratroop mission to rescue American prisoners from a North Vietnamese internment camp was "Operation Ivory Coast." President Houphouët-Boigny's Chief of Protocol phoned the Embassy and said, "Look, if you have to go around naming military operations after us, couldn't you name *successful* ones?"

Lately, Liberians, whose friendship with the United States used to be taken for granted regardless of how the United States acted toward them, have increasingly been voicing disenchantment with their big American brother. For one thing there was a flap over the eight-hundred-million-dollar, two-hundred-and-fifty-bed John F. Kennedy Memorial Medical Center in Monrovia, built with American aid money. It was visualized as a West African hospital specializing in tropical diseases, but while it was under construction the tropics got to it. Situated at the edge of the ocean, some of its delicate equipment and wiring was adversely affected by the salt air; there were other technical goofs and gaffes; and in December, 1970, just before the installation was to have been ceremoniously turned over to the Liberian government, Liberia brusquely refused to accept it. (It would be another six months before the donee could be persuaded to accept the donor's gift.)

At about the same time, the National Broadcasting Company put on a television documentary on Liberia, from which President Tubman and some his fellow Liberians got the impression that they were being mocked as clownish Uncle Toms. Now, if there is anything that galls Liberians, it is to have their formalism and love of ritual derided, to make them seem like buffoons in an old-fashioned musical comedy. They are intensely proud of their long-standing self-sovereignty, proud of their freedom, proud of their blackness. (No white person may become a Liberian citizen; on the other hand, any black can obtain citizenship in seventy-two hours.) "To many outsiders, much of what goes on here seems to be straight out of Octavus Roy Cohen," one American in Liberia told me. "But these people aren't mimicking anybody, unless it is their own fathers. This is their own culture, and it just happens to

73

resemble a minstrel show. Liberians know this, and they do the minstrel-show bit the way a white Southern politician talks Southern when it suits his purposes. Also, these Liberian blacks don't have to accommodate to any one else's ideas of behavior to achieve their political ends, because they already *have* black power. They tend to disapprove of black militants in the United States; their American heroes are more likely to be conservative blacks like Billy Simpson, the Washington restaurant-owner. When he visited Liberia, it was like a Kennedy visiting Ireland. What's more, the Amos-and-Andy stereotypes who in most people's minds represent Liberia actually comprise only two percent of the population. Sure, they sometimes act ridiculous by Western lights, but I think John O'Hara people are ridiculous, too, and they're probably only two percent of the American people."

The NBC documentary stressed the Amos-and-Andy side of Liberian life, and although it was never televised in Liberia, several government officials in Monrovia, including President Tubman, got hold of prints of the film and waved them angrily in American faces. The president himself, in his quarter of a century in office, had hardly ever uttered a word of public criticism against America, but now he told a story about how an American president, whom he did not name, had treated him discourteously. What had happened was that while an official visit to the States was being laid on for the Liberian president in 1954, and he had been asked if he had any special requests, he had said yes, there was one, he would like to see Franklin D. Roosevelt's grave at Hyde Park. In Washington, Secretary of State Dulles had astounded Tubman by saying there would have to be one change in his itinerary; that he couldn't make the trek after all because Franklin D. Roosevelt, Jr., was running for Attorney General of New York that November, and the Republican administration didn't want to risk having Tubman's Hyde Park pilgrimage perhaps cause Negroes in New York to identify more strongly than ever with the Democratic Party. So that part of Tubman's itinerary had been dropped, and a Hudson River cruise with Thomas E. Dewey was substituted.

"What sort of a country are you, anyway, playing politics like that with the man who for so many years was your best friend in

Africa?" a Liberian foreign-office man demanded of me, waving a
film can containing *his* print of the NBC show in my face. "We
are small and poor and can't do much about a giant land like
yours, but sometimes we feel that this giant needs psychiatric
treatment. The idea of going around hitting a mosquito with a
hammer! I would hope that when Africa finally emerges, as she is
bound to emerge, she won't have unpleasant recollections of you.
I can't help wondering whether your treatment of us, like the un-
truths you tell about us on your television, might not be intended
to turn your American Negroes against us, or whether your
Negroes might not be giving you so much trouble you have to find
another outlet for your rage."

Black Africans pay a good deal of attention to how black Americans are faring in America—much more than they pay to how
those few of them in Africa are faring there. For a while, after
independence, there was something of an influx of black Americans to the continent. Ghana, under Nkrumah, had a couple of
hundred of them in residence. It was a logical destination for
them; English is spoken, and Ghanaians look more like black
Americans than most other Africans. "This is where we came
from," one black American in Accra told me. "This is where our
brothers are." Now there are at most a few dozen black Americans
permanently residing in Ghana. Some who thought they might
spend the rest of their lives there have moved on. One Chicago
couple—he a maintenance man in a public-housing project, she
a nurse at an Illinois state hospital—migrated to Ghana with their
five children in 1966, penniless but hopeful. The wife began
baking doughnuts to earn some money, and in a year and a half
the couple had a flourishing small business, supplying box lunches
for more than a thousand construction workers at a rural factory
site. The Americans were about to branch out into an animal-feed
venture and other enterprises when they ran afoul of Ghanaian
xenophobia. So many inhibiting restrictions were imposed on alien
businessmen that even though the couple couldn't speak French,
they packed up and moved on to Togo, where they took over an
abandoned Peace Corps hostel and turned it into a small hotel.
There are probably only between five hundred and a thousand

permanent black American residents anywhere in Africa today. For many of the early arrivals, there was considerable disillusionment. Africans thought of them as Americans first and blacks second. Quite a few of the Americans were women who married Africans; the demands of the extended-family system so entrenched in Africa proved too much for them; it was one thing to choose to live with a single African; it was something quite different to be expected to live with, be guided by, and be responsible to, an entire clan. Some seventy-five black Hebrews from the United States set up a commune in Liberia in 1968. They stuck it out for two harrowing years and then departed for Israel; among their other handicaps was the fact that a good many Liberians had them confused with black Muslims. "The back-to-Africa movement is just about dead," I was told in Abidjan by a young American black woman who has stuck it out; born in Alabama and educated in New York, she went to Africa originally as a tourist, decided to stay, and is now employed by an Ivorian government ministry.

One runs into scattered other black Americans who have found their niche in Africa, but they are a small and special group—the former journalist in Harlem who accepted a teaching job in Ethiopia in 1945 largely because his grandmother, a freed slave who lived to be a hundred and thirteen, had enlivened his boyhood with tales of the continent of her birth; another schoolteacher, now in Zambia, who as a boy in Michigan, way back in the days when to call an American Negro an "African" was an insult, had dreamed of commanding a great black army that would free Africa from its colonial shackles; and the New Jersey man who moved to Africa following a prison term as a war protester, was married for a while to a Ghanaian, and ended up as a government adviser in Tanzania. Americans like these who have elected to make Africa their home (though none of the three aforementioned has given up his United States citizenship) are frequently sought out for counsel by newer arrivals, predominant among them young black militants from the States surprised by the coolness often shown them by Africans from whom they had expected ardent fraternal hugs.

"We can understand what drives some of your frustrated young blacks to come over here," one Ghanaian told me, "but we really aren't interested in hearing interminably about their racial hang-ups. After all, we have our own problems." And a Zambian said, "I spent an evening not long ago with a couple of chip-on-the-shoulder black American kids who were invited to dinner at the home of an American foreign-service man, who happens to be black himself, and the two of them took half the evening accusing me of professing to know more about the United States than they did, which, considering all the time I've spent in America, may be the case; and the other half telling their host that there was absolutely no difference between the United States and South Africa. I was delighted to hear a few days afterward that they'd got fed up with the generally low level of militancy in black Africa and had gone home."

There are a number of extremely capable black Americans—among them two ambassadors—currently representing the United States in Africa, and the angry young visitors tend to dismiss them, sometimes to their face, as Toms. One black American on a post-graduate fellowship arrived in Kenya and was amazed when, on approaching random Africans with hand outstretched and a hearty "Hi, Bro!" greeting, they politely stepped aside. "These guys just aren't with the black people," he said afterward. "They're just brainwashed! They're nothing but black Englishmen!"

Many of the heroes of black Americans are also hugely admired in Africa, and *their* welcome is warm indeed. When James Brown turns up—his records are heard everywhere, and nobody knows how many children have been named after him—he plays stadiums instead of theatres. He outdrew Hubert Humphrey in the Ivory Coast, even though the Minnesotan was vice-president at the time and was bearing a thirty-three-million-dollar foreign aid gift to that money-minded country. In Tanzania, Brown was a bigger attraction than a piece of the moon; in Mali, when the United States Information Service announced a showing of some Apollo XI lunar films, a big crowd turned out under the misapprehension that the presentation had something to do with James Brown at the Apollo Theatre. In Zambia, he was introduced at the State House by President Kaunda as Zambia's Soul Brother No. 1 (Brown diplomatically rejoined that no, the President was Soul

77

Brother No. 1, he was just No. 2); arriving at the airport at Lagos, he was all but mobbed by six thousand Nigerians, the largest crowd who had ever greeted anyone there.

Nigerians also showed up in droves on a less joyous occasion—the funeral in Lagos of Ralph Featherstone, the militant American who was killed when a bomb blew up in his car at the time of the H. Rap Brown trial in Nashville, Tennessee. Featherstone had once studied in Nigeria, and his widow brought his ashes back there for interment in what she called his symbolic home. The Featherstone funeral was one of the biggest in recent Nigerian history. There was some bewilderment that only his ashes had been brought home—cremation is most un-African—but there was also the strong feeling, notwithstanding the possibility that the lethal bomb was one Featherstone had made himself, that a brother slain by white American racists was coming back to the land of his origins for his final rest. There is no evidence that any Nigerians drew an ironic parallel between the death of Featherstone and that in Lagos of Whitney Young, Jr., whose body was flown in an Air Force plane for burial in the United States.

6

It comes as a shock to some black Americans visiting Africa for the first time to learn that their ancestors were not only slaves but slavers, too. At a recent symposium in Accra attended by both Ghanaians and black Americans, there was a spirited debate between the two groups—the indigenes contending that Africans who sold other Africans into slavery, like the kings of Abomey, who furnished a thousand bodies a month to European slave brokers, had to share the responsibility for the evil commerce, the visitors contending that no, black sellers couldn't be blamed, only white buyers. (While they were at it, the participating Americans took their hosts to task for tolerating the wearing of straight-hair wigs, long popular among Ghanaian women. Not long afterward, Afro wigs became the vogue in Accra, and soon spread all over the country—evidence of a sort of reverse cultural impact.)

Across the continent, in East Africa as well as West, there are sites whose historicity stems from slavery. Most of these are along the Gulf of Guinea. In Dahomey, for instance, there is Ouidah, a fortress built by Portugal in 1677 and manned as late as 1960, within the consent of the French colonial authorities, by a Portuguese garrison consisting of a single soldier. The hub of the slave trade was in the area that now is Ghana, where from the fifteenth century on, fifty forts and castles, most of them connected in one way or another with slavery, were erected by Portugal, Holland, England, Germany, France, Sweden, and Denmark. (Accra was once known as Christiansborg.) Ghanaians exhibit some ambivalence toward these grisly structures—one of them incongruously named Fort Patience—which have been called the Wailing Walls of Africa. The Ghanaians loathe their associations but regard them as potential lures for tourists, especially black American tourists. Some black Americans, among them Franklin H. Williams, President Johnson's ambassador to Ghana, have helped form the Africa Descendants Association, an Accra-based group that has been trying to collect money to restore one crumbling slave station, Fort Amsterdam, built by the Dutch in 1630 at Cormantin-Abandze, twenty miles east of Accra. The Association has been trying to raise funds from black Americans to reconstruct the dungeons in which their ancestors were chained, but has found it hard going; many black Americans don't want to be reminded of slavery, let alone memorialize it.

The driving force behind this shrine is a black American dentist in Accra, a South Carolinian whose parents chose to name him Robert E. Lee. "Every black has his history rooted in this slave thing," he says. Dr. Lee moved to Ghana from Brooklyn in 1955, built up a successful practice, and has taken out Ghanaian citizenship. He feels he has made a very self-satisfying cultural adjustment. "If I'd stayed in New York, I'd probably be practicing in a ghetto with nothing but black patients," he says. "Here I have patients from all over the world. If I were still living in New York, I'd probably be very explosive. Living here has toned down my philosophical content. What I like about Accra is that my children can fit into every element of society." One of his sons is a jet pilot in the Ghanaian Air Force.

Fort Amsterdam is just one of the many slave castles strung out along the edge of the Gulf of Guinea for sixty miles eastward of Accra. At the Cape Coast Castle, which is in better shape than Dr. Lee's fort, visitors who care for this sort of thing can inspect one set of wall hooks, from which male slaves were hung by their hands to weaken their bodies and spirits before they were placed on board a ship, and a second set of hooks for those who didn't seem sufficiently debilitated by twenty-five minutes on the first. Perhaps inspired by the example of the Africa Descendants Association, the Ghanaian government has lately been talking of refurbishing some of the old dungeons on its own, under the general auspices of the National Museum, in Accra, which already numbers among its exhibits a prime collection of neck chains and leg yokes. In its storerooms, the museum has many more such relics of the malign old days. Inasmuch as 1471 is the generally accepted date for the inauguration of the West African slave trade, Ghana thought it would be fitting to observe the five-hundredth anniversary of that business by converting the Cape Coast Castle into a regional slave museum and opening it up with a splash in 1971. The museum hired an ethnographer—a white ethnographer, as it happened—to take charge of the project, and he spent nearly two years drawing up plans and even designing labels for individual exhibits, but the money that was supposed to be forthcoming to implement the scheme somehow never got appropriated. Meanwhile, some of the castles go on crumbling, and others have been put to contemporary uses. The one at Elmina, built by the Portuguese in 1482, was supposedly visited by Columbus nine years later. He is said to have set his ship's compass by its compass, which, considering that he thought he was going to the East Indies and ended up in North America, may be no great shakes of a claim. At the Elmina castle, the morbid visitor can inspect the room where violent slaves were executed, the tunnel through which more docile ones were shepherded to the beach, and the ladder up which female slaves climbed to the governor's quarters. Just inside the dimly lit main entrance, the sharp-eyed visitor may spot a police circular on a bulletin board, complete with photograph: "WANTED For Conspiracy and Murder—Kwame Nkrumah." "Fond of bulletproof suits and Chinese attire," the circular details. "Believed to be armed." A nation's history takes curious turns.

Among the most eminent, and indisputably the most venerable, of all the black Americans who were attracted to Nkrumah's Ghana was Dr. William E. B. DuBois, who left the United States at the age of eighty-nine and died in Accra, a Ghanaian citizen, at ninety-four. He is buried on the State House grounds. At his death, he was compiling an *Encyclopedia Africana*. Upon Nkrumah's downfall, Dr. DuBois's editorial successors decided it would be awkward to have to include an account of the life of Ghana's disgraced liberator in the work in progress, so they decided to run biographies of dead Africans only, thus removing from their well earned place in recent African history, among others, Haile Selassie and Jomo Kenyatta.

Ghana's own place in African history has been unique. Some Africans regard it as a bellwether state. It is a nation that got rid of a civilian leader by means of a military coup, endured a military government, and then returned, in August, 1969, to civilian rule. As Ghana's independence was precedental, so, some other African nations profoundly hope, its political evolution will also prove to be. It is even a multiparty state. Prime Minister Busia's majority party holds one hundred and five of the one hundred and thirty seats in parliament, so the opposition does not constitute much of a threat.

Not that everyone is happy with the political situation in Ghana nowadays. Ghanaians who were delighted at the installation in power of Dr. Busia, a fifty-eight-year-old sociologist with an Oxford Ph.D., have lately been grumbling that perhaps Nkrumah wasn't after all *sui generis*, that perhaps all politicians of every stripe are corrupt, or high-handed, or both. Dr. Busia let it be known that he didn't intend to be bound by Supreme Court judgments he disagreed with, and he has seemed indifferent to a provision of the Ghanaian Constitution requiring the country's principal public servants, including the prime minister, to give a public accounting of their assets. When Busia arrived at the national university some months back, escorted by a fleet of Mercedes limousines, a student boldly asked him how a country that was so deep in debt could afford such a glittering cavalcade. The police promptly whisked him off and asked him a good many questions of their own. What particularly dismayed some Ghanaians about the incident was that when, later the same day, the prime minister happened to talk with some more students, nobody inquired about the arrest of the first one.

Still, one does not with impunity twit any African authority figure, and most Ghanaians find life much freer and easier than it was toward the end of the Nkrumah regime. "I'll tell you how bad it was under Nkrumah," one Ghanaian told me. "I was in London, complaining about the state of things in Ghana at a coffee house, when I looked up and saw a black man coming in. Now, he could have been a black man from anywhere, but he could also have been a Ghanaian, and—although the chances were a million to one—he could also have been a Ghanaian security man. So I quickly stopped talking. When people feel the way I felt then, *that* was repression."

As is the case elsewhere in Africa, Ghana might have fewer problems if it could provide more jobs. The government is the largest single employer, and pay rates are low—the equivalent of seventy-five cents a day being the legal minimum. Ghana had a comparatively strong trade-union movement, with three hundred and fifty thousand members in the Trade Union Congress, but the government abolished the group in 1971, charging its leader with "economic subversion" by fomenting illegal strikes. Since wages were meager, union dues thus miniscule, strikes forbidden, and government wages fixed by civil-service codes, it was difficult at best for the union to achieve much of a bargaining position. Moreover, employers in the private sector who probably could give their workers raises argued that they couldn't pay more than the government does because the government workers would then demand to have *their* wage codes changed, and this could lead to nationwide chaos; and the government, which had had its fill of unrest, was glad to throw its weight behind the private employers. There could conceivably be even worse unemployment as the result of the recent invention by one Ghanaian of an orange-peeling machine, for it seems at times as if half the women on the streets of Accra keep busy peeling oranges. It is hard to figure out who eats them all.

7

Africa is so big a continent that to try to cover more than a fraction of it, in a limited time, one is obliged to travel by air. While in Ghana, though, I decided to take my family by car on a six-hundred mile drive along the coast from Accra to Lagos, traversing Togo and Dahomey. I had been discouraged from going overland by a tourist agency I consulted in Accra, on the ground that some border guards behaved capriciously even if one held all the necessary visas, but I wanted to see something of the country-side, so I hired a car and driver notwithstanding. I never dreamed that the main obstacle to a serene passage would turn out to be the agency's own driver. Some African drivers have extraordinary eyesight. Later, in Uganda, we would find one who, while moving along at a brisk clip, would stop abruptly to call our attention to a green chameleon he had somehow spied clinging to an identical green leaf. Our Ghanaian driver, however, couldn't see approach-ing cars too well, and he was especially myopic about potholes, which in much of Africa are decidedly worth watching for.

Togo is a unique African country. French is the dominant language today, but the territory now included within its borders has within the past century been under the colonial sway of

Germany, France, and Britain. The Germans left, involuntarily, at the start of the First World War. They have come back. The West German diplomatic mission at Lomé is larger than the British, and Togo's frail economy has been given a recent boost by West German investments in harbor facilities, a textile mill, and, suitably, a brewery. Biere Benin has a robust European tang. Lomé has a population of one hundred and fifty thousand, nearly one-tenth of all the inhabitants of Togo, and it also has a woman mayor, Marie Sivomey. Now forty-seven, she became a French-colonial administrator at eighteen—the first female Togolese civil servant. Today, she is Togo's principal feminist, and she has been the head of the francophone branch (it goes without saying that there is also an anglophone branch) of the Council of West African Women. Her early life typifies the complexity of recent Togolese history. Her parents' only foreign language was German, and of their twelve children, some learned only English and others, like the Mayor, only French.

There were advantages, she thinks, in being brushed by three alien cultures, but there were also disadvantages; her father couldn't help his children with their homework. To Madame Sivomey's parents, the Germans were the finest people—white people, anyway—on earth. True, they were rather addicted to corporal punishment, but errant Togolese felt on the whole that twenty-five lashes was a less severe sentence than twenty-five days in jail. (Many Africans seem far abler than most other humans to withstand pain. They stoically endure tattooing and scarification; they accept grueling circumcision rites as a normal concomitant of puberty; while I was in Monrovia, and one taxi driver inadvertently slammed a trunk lid on another's hand, the victim didn't yell, but merely chided his friend for his carelessness and walked off to have the injury treated.) Whenever Madame Sivomey wanted to cajole her Teutonophile parents into giving her a special treat, she would look up what she wanted in a German dictionary and ask for it in German and get it.

During the Second World War, there were some difficult times within her family. Her parents were rooting for the Axis powers to win and their children for the Allies; it was a conflict of loyalties that also beset other Togolese families. Madame Sivomey, whose municipal powers are limited, since education, health, and law-and-order come under the federal government, has been mayor of Lomé since 1967. Ever since, as an enthusiastic supporter of the World Federation of Twin Cities, she has been trying to establish a sororal relationship with San Juan, Puerto Rico, and Bay City, Michigan, which the Federation in its mysterious ways has designated sister cities of Lomé. But the mayors of San Juan and Bay City, Madame Sivomey laments, never answer her letters. Maybe they think that "Lomé, Togo," is somebody's idea of a practical joke.

En route from Lomé to Cotonou, the capital of Dahomey, we were flagged down after dark by two flashlight-wielding Dahomeyan policemen, hunting smugglers. While they looked us over, our driver switched off his engine, and he had trouble starting it again. He assured us when we reached Cotonou that there was nothing wrong with the car and that it would be in fine shape the following morning to take us to Ganvié, the justly celebrated Dahomeyan village where twenty thousand people live on a lake in houses built on stilts, poling themselves about on neighborly calls in long, slim pirogues. In the morning, the driver picked us up, assured us that he knew the way to Ganvié, and drove off westward. I knew that Ganvié was to the north, but I assumed we'd be turning off in that direction at any moment. We traveled thirty miles, on the same road we'd covered coming from Lomé, before, on being pressed for a definite answer, the driver admitted he had no idea where the turnoff was. To calm me down and cheer me up, my wife quickly said that few westerners would probably get to know this particular stretch of road as well as I would; she added, in French, that I must not rebuke our man, lest he lose face.

Backtracking, we reached the spot where the police had stopped us the night before. There they were again, and I suggested gently to the driver that he stop so we could ask for directions. He braked so sharply that again he stalled, and this time the engine wouldn't kick over. The police tried to help, and the drivers of two other cars did their vain bit, while our man stood mutely by, opening his mouth only to say that he could probably fix whatever was wrong if he had a wrench, but that he didn't, although he was certain there had been one in the car when we left Accra. Finally

87

an Opel station wagon came along, with "Apollo XI" inscribed on it. The driver of Apollo's chariot pointed out to me that our car was also an Opel, and said he happened to know the best Opel mechanic in Cotonou, and would be glad to drive us there and introduce me to him. I dropped my wife and children at our hotel, and the Apollo man escorted me to the Opel mechanic, who was working with surgeonlike dedication on an engine. A moment after we arrived, he had it purring, and as soon as my intermediary had explained the situation to him, he grabbed his tool kit and set off with us.

Back at the scene of our breakdown, the cops had disappeared, and so, apparently, had our driver, who turned out to be asleep on the back seat. He spoke no French, and the master mechanic spoke no English, but it didn't matter. The mechanic never even looked at the part of our engine that the driver seemed to think was defective. Instead, he began to dismantle the distributor, using his hands, his shirt, his mouth. Never had an Opel been so tenderly disassembled, or so thoroughly. There were parts strewn all over the shoulder of the road. Finally the mechanic put everything together again. The engine started up at once. With a final, disdainful thrust at my driver, the mechanic filled the near-empty radiator with some water from a bucket that a passing Dahomeyan boy had magically produced. Heading back to Cotonou, we were flagged down by the two policemen, who it turned out wanted this time merely to extend their felicitations on our providential deliverance. We exulted together, in a torrent of international good will, while the driver sulked. When we got back to the Opel garage, a man came along on a motor bike and kissed the mechanic on both cheeks. I felt like doing that myself, but confined myself to a large *pourboire* and the silent reflection that I had not long before had far more trouble getting a car repaired when it broke down in the middle of Manhattan Island.

Dahomey is incredibly poor, though there is a three-million-dollar presidential palace in Cotonou. Until 1965, its only export to the United States was postage stamps. Now the country exports a little palm oil, and it hopes to increase bilateral trade with its big neighbor Nigeria. Dahomey has suffered from a peculiar backlash of independence. In the colonial days, the French had a high opinion of the administrative skills of Dahomeyans. They educated an unusually high percentage of them and sent them all over West Africa to fill bureaucratic posts. No one knows if Dahomeyans are inherently superior to other West Africans—perhaps they inherited some special authoritative bent from their ruthless kings—but the French *thought* they were, and stationed them far and wide, until they spread over francophone Africa far beyond their proportionate numbers. Then xenophobia came along, and one by one they were declared surplus in Niger or Senegal or wherever, and they drifted back home, whereupon their own government felt obliged to put them on the payroll. Now, seventy percent of Dahomey's national budget goes for salaries. The care and feeding of repatriates is merely one aspect of this; another is that there have been frequent changes of government, and with each change new jobs have had to be created, since practically nobody gets fired. At the moment, Dahomey has a troika presidency—three men, each an ex-president of the country, each in turn serving one-third of a six-year term. And for the entire six years each has his own personal staff. All three members of the triumvirate attend cabinet meetings, and they all turn up at public functions; if any one fails to show, there is instant speculation over the reason for his dereliction. Yet for all this bizarre multiplicity of leadership, some Africanists have been wondering if perhaps in the long run little Dahomey may not prove to be more stable than some of the larger African nations committed inflexibly to the domination of a single, powerful, and, obviously, mortal leader. Dahomeyans themselves are unperturbed by their complicated setup, and they are proud that their last coup d'état was, for a country with such sanguinary traditions, remarkably bloodless; many people in Cotonou weren't aware that it had taken place until it was all over.

In Dahomey, as in most of Africa, witchcraft is still widely practiced and respected. Nearly every public market on the continent has its juju stalls, offering dead birds, dead rats, monkeys' paws, and powders and potables galore. Soccer teams in Kenya hire witch doctors to keep their players healthy and, if possible, to hex the opposition. In Abidjan, I fell into conversation with a sophisticated Ivorian woman, educated in Paris, well-read and well-traveled, who got to recounting an old legend about a onetime

African queen who, to lead her people across a crocodile-infested river, sacrificed one of her children to the reptiles, whereupon some hippopotamuses promptly lined up and formed a bridge over which the royal party could safely pass. When I asked if many contemporary Africans put much stock in the yarn, she said, "You can't be African and not believe it."

Tolerating the rituals of fetishers is not always conducive to the national health, but the national leaders are wary of taking too strong a stand against this, lest they damage the national morale. At the same time that the Tanzanian government was inveighing against rural practitioners whose clumsy methods of circumcision had resulted in more than fifty deaths, placards were displayed at the main market in Dar es Salaam urging passersby to patronize witch doctors. "You will get cured may be," one sign said. Some conventional doctors in Africa with degrees from American or European medical schools will not even attempt to treat patients who are supposed to be under a curse. Nowhere is witchcraft taken more seriously than in Dahomey. On the road to Abomey one day, a companion pointed out a big shade tree with a score of sticks thrust into the ground beneath it; if somebody wants you to have an accident and plants a stick there dedicated to you, my Dahomeyan acquaintance said soberly, you will have an accident. The French ambassador in Cotonou is reliably thought by the rest of the diplomatic corps to have a close working relationship with the best fetisher in town. As evidence, they point out that it never rains on the Fourteenth of July, but since the American ambassador does not much go in for this sort of thing, it almost always rains on the Fourth.

In Cotonou, a friend invited my family and me to attend an evening session at the house of one of the dozen or so full-time fetishers in that city of some seven hundred and fifty thousand. This witch doctor, a man apparently in his mid-thirties, had inherited his father's practice, and had the reputation of being not only able to cure most diseases, but, if he was in the mood, to transmit German measles—just about the only ailment we hadn't been inoculated against. But the risk of catching that seemed smaller than the risk of driving to Nigeria with a Ghanaian driver and not taking all possible precautions. Our escort warned us in advance that if the fetisher should happen to warn us not to undertake the trip on a particular day, we should by no means ignore him; to do so would be worse than having a stick planted under a roadside tree.

About one hundred Dahomeyans, including a band, were gathered in the fetisher's dark courtyard when we arrived. The witch doctor, clad in a robe and a snakeskin hat embellished with cowrie shells, jingled a cowbell for attention and then dipped cola nuts into a bowl of water and passed them around. The water didn't look especially clean, and neither did the fetisher's hand, but to refuse a cola nut in Africa is to reject a traditional gesture of hospitality, so we shrugged and chewed; we *had* had cholera shots, and a cola nut seemed an unlikely source of German measles.

Then we were invited into his living quarters, a room perhaps twelve by twenty feet, lit by kerosene lanterns, and decorated with, among other icons, photographs of a pin-up girl and of General Gowon of Nigeria, with a legend on it that incorporated both a pun and an acrostic: "Go On With One Nigeria." A dozen or so disciples stood around, and two of them, teenage girls with white paste smeared on their faces, soon went into trances and walked around jerkily, slapping and tugging at the rest of us. The witch doctor sat on the dirt floor, pounded on his bell with the edge of a knife, presumably to summon his spirits, and then began to toss a handful of pebbles in front of him, as if he were shooting craps. Told by an interpreter that we would be driving to Lagos, he did not specify any particular day to go, or not go, but he said if we arrived safely we were to send him fifteen hundred francs—about four dollars—and a bottle of gin. Told next that a young American girl in our group was studying for an exam, he guaranteed her a mark of 100 if she would send him two hundred cola nuts or two thousand francs, and added, without mentioning a fee, that she was in danger of being impregnated by a man who would refuse to marry her. The girl's mother was present, and gasped. The fetisher gave me a small cloth talisman to take along on our journey, which seemed a bargain at a thousand francs; I decided impulsively also to pay him the other fifteen hundred on the spot, as a kind of insurance. After a final warning to my wife and me that if we touched each other in bed that night we should be careful not to touch the talisman the following morning, the fetisher announced that his spirits were about to depart, and a few minutes later, a puff of smoke from somewhere signified that they had taken their leave. So, while he danced around his courtyard, a fetish doll in one hand, his cowbell in the other, we took our leave as well.

At the Dahomey side of the Nigerian border there was a small building marked "Hall of Tourism." It was abandoned, and seemed somehow symbolic of its country's economic plight. At the border itself, a Dahomeyan immigration man was boldly asking all transients for money. I gave him three hundred francs, and with a broad smile he waved us on into Nigeria. The Nigerian immigration and customs procedures proved to be something else again. I learned then, for the first time, that our driver, whose calling card described him as an "administrative technical assistant," had fallen short of his efficient description of himself. He, a Ghanaian, from the very country that not long before had rudely repatriated ten thousand Nigerians and thus incurred considerable Nigerian animosity, had arrived at the border without a Nigerian visa. When the Nigerian official on duty asked why he had neglected to obtain one, the Ghanaian said lamely that he had forgotten to. Visas are important in Nigeria; since the Biafran War, the government has been issuing them warily. I myself had obtained fifteen-day visas for my family back in Washington, but even so I had been somewhat nervous about entering the country, having heard of another American with a bona fide visa who'd been turned back at the Lagos airport after flying all the way from New York. And here was the Ghanaian saying he'd forgotten! And after I had worried about his losing face!

It was just after six in the afternoon, and the gates to Dahomey had been shut for the night behind us, and Lagos lay fifty miles ahead, and now the Nigerian official began to give the Ghanaian a lecture—neatly blending sarcasm with contempt, rage with scorn, on behalf of all clean-living Nigerians putting all scoundrelly Ghanaians squarely in their miserable place. To this day I have no idea whether it was because of my fetisher's talisman or because in addition to our visas I had with me a letter of introduction from the Nigerian ambassador in Washington, but after another few minutes of general assessment, and debasement, of the driver's character and behavior, the Nigerian finally granted him a forty-eight-hour visa, warning him that if he didn't get out of the country at the end of that period what the merciless Kings of Abomey had done to their victims would by comparison seem like child's play. A few hours later we reached Lagos, and I bade the driver a curt goodbye. Not quite curt enough, it developed; we had barely checked into our rooms when he was on the phone: He had just cashed a traveler's check in the lobby, he told me, and wondered if I would like to exchange some Nigerian pounds for dollars. I decided not to send the fetisher his bottle of gin.

8

Under colonialism, black Africans had two principal objectives. Politically, they wanted self-government; economically, self-sufficiency. They got the first with surprising ease, all things considered; they are pursuing the second with rather more difficulty than they anticipated. As they emerged into independence, they believed that before they could attain much political *or* economic stability they would considerably have to jack up the educational level of their people. It was the men with the academic credentials, they had observed, who often seemed to win out in the world, whatever their color or continent. Indeed, some of the African leaders had got where they were simply by virtue of having been lucky enough to go off to school while their brothers continued to tend cassava patches or herds of cattle. Most Africans, though, had been left far in the ruck in the academic competition.

At independence time in the larger of the two Congos, that country of twenty million had just twelve college graduates. The turmoil that rocked the Congo for the first six years of its theoretical self-sovereignty stemmed at least partly from its not having enough people around trained in the complexities of managing more than a single family's affairs. When the Congo became independent, among its nativity gifts from the United States were four hundred college-level scholarships. The recipient had a hard time finding enough qualified high-school graduates to fill them. Now, a decade later, the educational picture there has brightened a bit. The Congo has eleven hundred college graduates—about one twentieth of one percent of its population—and three universities of its own, with a total enrollment, when they are functioning, of nearly seven thousand.

Even those new African nations with a comparatively large number of college graduates weren't as well off at independence time as they seemed to be: The one place in which educated Africans often seemed loath to apply their expertise was Africa. On many a university campus in the United States, in England, and on the European continent, clusters of Africans could be found in close to tribal strength—men and women pursuing higher education with calculatedly laggard steps, reluctant to return home because of political instability or economic uncertainty or merely because they found the cultivated alien groves of academe more pleasant than the thorny savannahs or rank rain forests of their fatherlands.

Today, the absentees are not so sorely missed. Indeed, so many educated men and women are being turned out by schools and colleges and universities *in* Africa that, across a continent still dominated by agriculture, their professional and technical skills are not always usable. At the same time that Tanzania, like most of its neighbor nations, is trying to train its own people to replace expatriates in managerial jobs, it is beginning to wonder just how far an agricultural country should go in creating a class of urban educated elite. President Julius Nyerere, himself a teacher, is so persuaded of the importance of rural life in the Tanzanian scheme of things that he has been using every means he can think of— including summary roundups and rustications—to get Tanzanians out of the cities and into the country, where he is convinced their future lies. "Instead of the primary school activities being geared to the competitive examination which will select the few who go on to secondary school, they must be a preparation for the life which the majority of children will lead," he has said. "At present, our pupils learn to despise even their own parents because they are old-fashioned and ignorant; there is nothing in our existing educational system which suggests to the pupil that he can learn important things about farming from his elders. The result is that he absorbs beliefs about witchcraft before he goes to school, but does not learn the properties of local grasses; he absorbs the taboos from his family, but does not learn the methods of making nutritious traditional foods. And from school he acquires knowledge unrelated to agricultural life. He gets the worst of both systems!"

The feeling has spread throughout black Africa that old-fashioned education, once so coveted, is perhaps no longer the cure-all for the continent's woes. Thoughtful Africans are beginning to wonder about the obscure long-term value of universal free secondary, or even primary, education, when its all too visible short-term results seem to be the presence in African cities of disenchanted swarms of the newly educated, who can't find urban employment and to whom it would be mortifying, as new-hatched members of the community of scholars, to return to the bush and pick up a hoe. In Ethiopia, only a generation ago, parents had to be all but bribed to permit their sons to become students instead of shepherds; the government, with almost more schoolrooms than pupils, provided alluring incentives, and the Emperor himself would turn up every so often with cookies or other treats to keep the students from going home. Now, there are plenty of Ethiopians eager to go to school, but those who have been handed sheepskins do not as yet find suitable career opportunities as easily as those who can handle sheep.

Nonetheless, education remains the African dream. A Kenyan will pay ten thousand shillings (three hundred dollars) for a wife with a university degree. (In a recent beauty contest, the lucky young lady designated "Miss Kenya" was a Junior Research Fellow at the Social Science Division of the Institute for Development Studies at the University of Nairobi.) Twenty-five percent of Nigeria's federal budget is earmarked for education. (In the United States, it is four percent.) For many of the new countries, a national university, regardless of whether or not it makes sense educationally, has become a *sine qua non* of independence.

The colonialists, not unreasonably, thought in terms of regional

97

universities. Thus the French established the University of Dakar, to serve francophone West Africa; thus the British established the University of Makerere, in Uganda, to serve the anglophone East. But after independence, as the popularity of chauvinism came into conflict with the potentiality of cooperation, some educational institutions got caught in the crossfire. The Makerere campus was to have been transformed, by Uganda, Kenya, and Tanzania, into a University of East Africa, for all three countries. But there were too many jealousies, too many rivalries, and since the summer of 1970 each of the three has had its own establishment. Earlier, when the British had decided that their principal *West* African institution for the edification of anglophone natives should be at Ibadan, Nigeria, the Ghanaians in what was then the Gold Coast were miffed and instituted a university of their own. It was at Legon, on the outskirts of Accra, and they helped support it by a surtax on every outgoing bag of cocoa, the area's principal export. Today, some Ghanaians consider it vindication of their stubbornness and self-confidence that the recently formed Association of African Universities, which has forty-two members, has made Accra its headquarters.

Under the colonialists, whatever higher education was obtainable in Africa was patterned on European curricula. The African establishments were unabashedly imitative, and when they seemed to succeed they measured that success in European terms; accordingly, Makerere became known as the Oxford of Africa, Dakar as the continent's Sorbonne. The British were on the whole more enthusiastic than the French: Dickens is more widely known in Africa than Dumas, though some of the younger Africans wonder why anybody on the continent should care a hoot about either of them. But for all the relative concern of the British, in absolute terms, their accomplishments were less than breathtaking. Zambia had just a hundred college graduates at independence, which put it well ahead of the once Belgian Congo but so far behind where Kenneth Kaunda thinks it should have been that the Zambian President has declared, "As far as education is concerned, Britain's record is most criminal." Britain wanted mainly to train junior bureaucrats to take over the tiresome administration, on lower levels, of what were known as "native affairs." France, which had no intention of delegating administrative control at any echelon, wanted to convert selected Africans into French-speaking, francophile, black quasi-Frenchmen. The Belgians, for their part, discouraged the education of any Congolese except those who professed a hankering for the priesthood.

At all the universities, there were so few Africans qualified to serve on faculties that most of the instruction had to be given by expatriates. That is still the case. The chief recruiters, reimbursers, and occupants of college-or-higher-level academic posts in independent Africa today are British and French. But the ratio between non-Africans and Africans is diminishing, and today in black Africa—it was not so a few years ago—there is not a single head of a university who is white. The universities are largely run by vice-chancellors; the chancellor is conventionally the chief of state. The credentials of some of the vice-chancellors would seem to be political rather than academic. The incumbent at the University of Dar es Salaam was, until he took that job, the secretary general of Tanzania's ruling political party. But others have impeccable scholarly backgrounds. At the University of Ghana, for instance, there is Alexander Kwapong, who took over in 1966. He has a double-first in Classics from Cambridge, where he also got a Ph.D. in ancient history; he taught the Classics for a year at Princeton. Then, until he moved to Geneva to become Assistant Director General of the World Health Organization, there was Dr. A. Thomas Lambo, the vice-chancellor at the University of Ibadan, who was West Africa's first black professor of psychiatry. Nigerian universities seem to attract medical men. The vice-chancellor of the University of Zaria is a pediatrician, the vice-chancellor of Nsukka University an ophthalmologist.

Dr. Lambo took up his profession largely by default. Under the British, the prestige fields for ambitious young Africans were law and medicine. He had an older brother who went into law, so that left medicine. He would have preferred to be a social anthropologist, and as a psychiatrist has spent much of his time looking into the effect of environment on human behavior. One of his studies revealed that there appeared to be little difference between neuroses regardless of environment: A rural African who had just been bewitched or whose wife had just been stolen had anxieties not discernibly different from those of a white-collar WASP in Manhattan who had lost his job or thought his heart was acting up.

African students are not immune to ideology. "Western imperialism" to many of them is not a verbal bogey plucked from Marxist dialectic but something very real that their parents successively suffered under, rose up against, and got rid of. Moreover, as youthful citizens of young nations, some of the students have naturally been curious about relatively young political systems. Quite a few Africans, by now, have studied at Lumumba University in Moscow, an experience about which they tend to have mixed feelings. For every one who returns acclaiming the Russians as the only true friends of the oppressed and downtrodden, there seems to be another who has contrary reminiscences: the Congolese back from Leningrad, for instance, whose white wife some Soviets tried to evict from their hotel room under the misapprehension that she was a Russian fooling around with a black visitor.

After independence, relations between the new African countries and the Soviet Union were for a while generally cozy, but then some of the Africans began to weary of the friendship. It was so joyless, so heavyhanded, so demanding of attention and energy. At the same time, Africans were quite aware that it was almost exclusively the Communist countries that were assisting the black liberation groups harassing the whites in southern Africa. Because young Africans are grateful for such foreign aid, and because teasing the United States has become a popular sport everywhere on earth, there are always Africans of student age willing to peddle "Leninism Today" to passersby outside the United States Information Service Library at Ibadan. Or, when it comes to that, to circulate on university campuses tracts of their own composition with such sentiments as "it would be dwelling in infantile illusions to think that this change from being exploited to embarking upon the path of socialist development can be achieved with the unqualified consent of, or co-operation with, capitalist monopolies or their vicious military machine. Therefore, the fundamental prerequisite for uplifting the living conditions of the masses through socialism is the disengagement, political and economic, from this system."

As students of the early 1970s go, however, the African ones—

allowing for the usual exceptions—are rather subdued. Dr. Lambo, while vice-chancellor at Ibadan, told me one time, "In black Africa today, there simply are no deep ideological or philosophical differences. Most young people are eager to learn, and they spend most of their time studying. I always say, 'Don't worry about our going Communist. Our culture runs against it. We may live communally, but we're imperialistic in terms of our acquisitiveness.' Oh, we have our demonstrations about Guinea or Vietnam, but these are largely pro forma. When the students around here break a British window or burn an American flag, it's mainly to show the rest of the community, and to satisfy themselves, that they're not square."

When Dr. Lambo's university had to be closed down, in February, 1971, after a student was shot to death by the police during a campus flare-up, the controversial issue had nothing to do with ideology; it stemmed from an undergraduate demand for the ouster of a cafeteria manager. Most African students toe the line because their future depends on their successfully completing their education and because the government pays in full for that education, including pocket money. Even when Africans attend universities located in their home cities, they usually become boarding students; many African houses simply don't have the space—or, often, the electricity—necessary for doing homework. Most student discontent, accordingly, relates to living conditions.

When I went to call on Vice-Chancellor Kwapong, in Ghana, he apologized for being thirty-five minutes late: He had been meeting with his students, who were in a fractious mood partly because a girls' dormitory wanted to hold a dance on a night on which a boys' dorm had already scheduled one, and partly because both sexes suspected refectory employees of taking students' food home to their families. "Most of the complaints here start with catering," Dr. Kwapong said. When, in Nigeria, I called on Dr. S. O. Biobaku, the vice-chancellor of the University of Lagos, he had not long before weathered a storm provoked by an insufficiency of accommodations for day students who wanted to become boarders. "I learned a lesson," he said. "Don't admit students until you have enough beds for them."

In handling disruptive students, African authorities have fewer compunctions than some elsewhere about getting tough. Presented with some student demands, President Tubman of Liberia brusquely said, "The hell with them." Following a complaint by a university publication in Ethiopia about the lack of civil liberties in that country at the end of 1969, more than a dozen students were shot to death by the police. Subsequently, to discourage spontaneous uprisings, students were informed they would have to give fifteen days' advance notice of any demonstration. In Nairobi, after the police had clubbed some students during a fracas arising from dissatisfaction with room assignments and the organization of the library, one newspaper editorial remarked that "it ought to be painfully clear to students by now that student ultimata are not worth the pieces of paper on which they are usually scrawled. And the simple reason is that no student body today in Africa possesses the sanctions necessary to back up threats against authority. Students are admitted to university, are maintained at university, and often employed after university, at public expense. It is a naive person indeed who cannot discern where power lies in this kind of situation." In the Congo, in June, 1969, the police were supposed to fire over the heads of some university students marching from their campus toward Kinshasa to protest about food and transportation. The policemen's aim was poor, or maybe good. In any event, they killed a dozen young people. Two years later, students staged a mock funeral for the victims. This time, the government shut down the university, and gave the three thousand-odd young men attending it three days either to sign up for a two-year hitch in the army or face charges of desertion. Sixteen men who refused to enlist were subsequently sentenced by a court martial to ten years' imprisonment. Most of the others were permitted to return to their studies, though technically still in the army, in September. In the Ivory Coast, when some five hundred university students were deported by President Houphouët-Boigny—in this instance there was no bloodshed—after trying to demonstrate outside the embassies of NATO countries, the government-controlled daily paper at once ran whole pages of testimonials to the president's action, one of them bearing the eight-column-wide headline *"Tout le pays approuve les mesures prises par le chef d'état."* Houphouët-Boigny himself told me, "We need unity in Africa, and we cannot tolerate opposition to that. I have no objection to students amusing themselves by shouting 'A *bas Colonialistes!*' or 'A *bas Imperialistes!*' But to demonstrate at embassies—no! We need harmonious development in Africa, and there can be no special rights for the young. They must act in accord with the public interest."

I spent an hour at the University of Dakar one day with a sad, gentle, perplexed Frenchman, who had been teaching English there for sixteen years. He felt out of tune with the times. He had two broken windows in his office; the students were in tune. They had been demonstrating for better dormitories and against French professors like himself, who comprised seventy percent of the senior faculty and whose salaries were paid by France. The students were fed up with being taught more about Charlemagne than about the heroes of African history. They had also been boycotting the classes of a visiting American professor; some said this was because he wasn't fluent in French, others because he was a Jew in a largely Muslim country.

When France built the university, in 1951, the professor said, the idea had been that the student body would be one-third French, one-third Senegalese, and one-third non-Senegalese African. Now the balance had shifted, and close to seventy percent of the students were Senegalese. The professor had formerly been a dean. In that capacity, he said, he had made a point of talking to students at least once a fortnight, and had given them free access to a campus bulletin board: why, he had even once arranged to have a door unlocked for them and thus saved them an extra half-mile walk to their refectory. But little things like that no longer seemed to satisfy them, and he was gloomy about the future prospects of the Sorbonne of the South. (At least Dakar had been living up to its name; when student dissension in Paris got the Sorbonne shut down in 1968, sympathetic student dissension in Dakar had brought about the identical result there.)

"When I came here in 1954," the professor said, "we had clubs —English and Spanish and so on—and we had dances and Christmas parties, and I knew all the students by their first names. But now we have no Christmas party, and we can't have meetings, because the students break them up. In 1969, an American Negro lawyer came here to make a speech, and the students wouldn't listen to him. One person in his party had a camera smashed, and another got slammed against a wall so hard he fractured both wrists. We've tried to make concessions to students' demands, but it's hard to figure out just what they want. Last year, we spent hundreds of hours on curriculum reform. My own field is fifteenth-century English literature, but I found a new course that I hoped would be relevant today—one on the evolution of English-speaking countries in Africa. But they weren't much interested. Sometimes, their protests seem nihilistic. Perhaps it all boils down to the fact that they don't want a university anymore that's run by Frenchmen like me. In any event, the spirit that used to animate this place is gone."

9

There would be far fewer educated Africans of any sort today save for the groundwork laid, under colonialism, by the Christian missionaries. As they went, schools went. The reason that most educated Ghanaians were traditionally up-country men was not because the northerners had any superior innate intelligence but because the missionaries couldn't bear the climate along the Guinea Coast. By the same token, though for a different reason, southern Nigerians are on the whole better educated than their northern brothers: the missionaries were tolerated, if not exactly welcomed, in the animist south, but were spurned by the largely Muslim north. Two of Africa's pre-eminent contemporary leaders, the Catholic Nyerere of Tanzania and the Protestant Kaunda of Zambia, were missionary-educated. Kaunda's father was a missionary himself. There are alternative ways of writing the principal language of Burundi—the French-Catholic-missionary way and the British-American-Protestant-missionary way. Africans are chary about contributing to most organized charities—philanthropy was not widely taught by anyone—but they can be counted on to help YMCA fund drives.

As elsewhere on earth, the missionaries in Africa met with

formidable resistance. They could never make much headway in stopping polygamy: African women slightly outnumber men, and in much of the continent it is a disgrace not to be married. Perhaps, all in all, the missionaries opened more minds than they saved souls. "We need a lot more teachers here," an indigenous Jesuit priest in the Congo told me, "but we don't need any more priests, and we need bishops even less." It was raining, and he looked up at the sky and added wryly, "If we were *real* believers, like our ancestors in the villages, we could stop the rain."

The missionaries are still much in evidence. There are one hundred and forty-three American private citizens living in Burundi today; one is a businessman and the others are Protestant missionaries. The plane I took to Africa had close to that number of Jehovah's Witnesses on board, setting forth on a one-month tour of African Kingdom Halls. A female Witness sitting alongside me, on the long pilgrimage from Kennedy to Dakar, told me all about Noah and the flood, when she was not singing hymns, and she pressed on me a copy of "The Truth That Leads to Eternal Life," published by the Watch Tower Bible & Tract Society of Pennsylvania; not knowing I was a writer, she may have wondered why I gasped on reading, inside, "First Edition, 15,000,000 Copies."

My seatmate said that Africa was not always an easy continent for the Witnesses. Since they are not permitted to salute temporal flags or sing terrestrial anthems, they get pushed around a good deal by nationalists. Her group had canceled a scheduled visit to Cameroon because, she said, the government had outlawed the Witnesses there, thus giving the rest of the citizenry free rein, she added matter-of-factly, to eat them.

The desire so prevalent in Africa today to Africanize institutions inherited from the colonialists has inevitably affected the continent's attitudes toward the old-time religions. The traditional Western-oriented sects are presently competing for converts with close to five thousand independent African-oriented churches, which all together have perhaps nine million disciples. While I was in Kinshasa, I spent some time with the largest of these, the Kimbanguists—formally, the Church of Jesus Christ on Earth Through the Prophet Simon Kimbangu. This church alone claims a membership of three million. It is the only church in Africa not founded by outside missionaries that has been accorded the distinction, consequential in Christian circles, of full-fledged recognition by the World Council of Churches, in Geneva.

Simon Kimbangu was a run-of-the-mill Congolese Baptist until, during the flu epidemic of 1918, he had a vision and heard a voice. He let the experience simmer for three years. Then in 1921 he began preaching and faith-healing. He soon attracted enough followers to prompt the very straitlaced Catholic Belgian colonial authorities to clap him in jail. They kept him there until his death, thirty years later. They banned his movement, and they exiled his principal adherents to remote parts of the territory. That proved to be tactically unsound, for clandestine pockets of Kimbanguism sprang up everywhere. In 1957, six years after Kimbangu's death, with independence for the Congo clearly in the offing, his followers emerged and presented the colonial Governor General with a dramatic alternative: Either he should grant them religious freedom, or execute them. The government let them function openly, and in December, 1959, moreover, let them remove Kimbangu's remains from a prison graveyard and ceremoniously reinter them at Nkamba, his birthplace, in Katanga province—now a Kimbanguist shrine renamed Nkamba-Jerusalem.

Kimbanguism has been denounced by Catholics and some Protestants in Africa as a holy-roller cult with overtones of witchcraft and God knows what all else. But the World Council thought otherwise, and in April, 1971, in part to demonstrate their regularity, the Kimbanguists embraced Communion. Unarguably Congolese in origin, Kimbanguism is chiefly heterodox in its differences with its environment. The Congo is a loud, volatile, uninhibited country. Kimbanguism is mild, low-keyed, and puritanical. Its followers are strictly enjoined from smoking, drinking, and polygamy. They may not even bathe naked. In a land, furthermore, where warfare has lately been a hallmark, they are unbending pacifists, and they have so much political influence that the last few national governments have all agreed not to send Kimbanguist soldiers into combat zones. I met one Kimbanguist—in his nonreligious life, a science teacher in a government high school —who had been an army officer from 1962 to 1968, when there

107

was much military action in the Congo, but he never saw any of it.

Social welfare and education are the sect's principal concerns. The Kimbanguists say that six hundred thousand students are enrolled in schools they run. (In that respect, they do not yet constitute much of a numerical threat to the Catholics, who have long controlled education in the Congo, and who today supervise the education of three-fifths of Congolese children.) For all their austerity, the Kimbanguists are fond of music. They have a brass band in Kinshasa of uncommon loudness and endurance. Green is the Kimbanguist color, and the band, in bright green uniforms, is a feature of most church functions. When there are no functions, it plays in the courtyard at the home of the leader of the movement, Joseph Diangenda.

Born in 1918, Diangenda is the youngest of three sons of Simon Kimbangu, who before his death named Joseph to carry on after him. Each of the two older brothers is active in the church and is known as "His Greatness." Joseph is called "His Eminence," and whenever Kimbanguists are in his presence, indoors or out, they remove their shoes as a mark of respect. When they approach him to talk, they kneel at his side. A short, squat man who usually wears a plain bush jacket, he is quite worldly; since independence, he has been to Ireland and Israel, and also, in 1965, to the United States, where he has a few followers. He has a cathedral in one suburb of Kinshasa, and in another has a large school building under construction. It has been going up by bits and pieces since 1967. The first Sunday of every month, his indefatigable band blaringly at his side, he holds all-day services on a clearing alongside the unfinished structure. There is some preaching, but most of the day is given over to fund-raising for the building. For eight or nine hours, without letup, several thousand Kimbanguists shuffle shoeless across the dusty ground in a sedate snake dance, waving handkerchiefs in time to the band music, dropping offerings into a white porcelain bowl placed on a table behind which sits His Eminence, protected from the sun by, of all peculiar shields, an umbrella advertising Haig Whiskey. On a routine first-of-the-month Sunday, the collection adds up to about ten thousand dollars.

Kimbanguism has by now spread to nine countries, so Papa Joseph, as His Eminence is sometimes familiarly called, does considerable traveling within Africa, too. He skips Angola, where the Portuguese authorities consider his movement as distasteful as the Belgians did a generation ago. Kimbanguists in Kinshasa allege that one hundred of their people were killed in Catholic Angola in 1970 alone, on the ground of being affiliated not with an African religious movement but, rather, with an international political conspiracy. By their very numbers, Diangenda's followers constitute a force to be reckoned with in the Congo, but it is hard to visualize them or their mild-mannered leader as a threat to the status quo anywhere. He himself has shown a remarkable facility for straddling the political gulf across the Congo River—with Brazzaville, the capital of the smaller, more radical, once French, People's Democratic Republic of the Congo on its west bank; and on its east, conservative Kinshasa, where the river, like the big country through which it meanders, is now formally called "Zaire." There are many Kimbanguists in Brazzaville, and their leader has had no difficulty getting across to minister to their spiritual needs and accept their offerings. Until recently, few others could make the half-mile journey with the same ease. All Kinshasa women, for instance, were forbidden to cross over, when their government became piqued at an allegation in Brazzaville that many of the commuters were prostitutes.

For a while, after both Congos became independent, they enjoyed reasonably amicable relations, but this detente ended in October, 1968. A man named Pierre Mulele, the instigator of an abortive 1964 rebellion in the larger Congo, had taken refuge in Brazzaville. He had crossed to Kinshasa four years later, under the impression he had been amnestied. Instead, on arrival, he was executed. Brazzaville took this as a glaring breach of trust, and the two countries severed relations. A ferry that traversed the river continued to operate, some of the time, but there were complications as to just who, the Kimbanguist leader aside, could use it. A few diplomats could, but only those—the British and Canadian ambassadors among them—who were accredited to both Congos. The United States, though it has never formally severed diplomatic relations with Brazzaville, has had no diplomatic *presence* there since 1965, when the American Embassy was subjected to a left-wing attack. The mission there asked for protection, and the Brazzaville government said it couldn't provide any. So the Americans departed, and in subsequent dealings we have used the West German mission as our go-between. (Brazzaville, incidentally, is the only capital city on earth where West and East Germany have simultaneously deployed diplomatic teams.) In June, 1970, the two Congos began gingerly to move toward a rapprochement. Their presidents met on shipboard halfway across the river, and seven months later formal relations were resumed. Washington and Brazzaville remained aloof.

Nearly every one in black Africa agrees that its three most populous cities are Lagos and Ibadan in Nigeria, and Kinshasa in the Congo, each with more than a million inhabitants. City limits and censuses being imprecise, however, no one is quite certain which is the biggest. Lagos and Ibadan are authentically African cities, pulsating with an African beat. Kinshasa, formerly Leopold-ville, is an authentically Belgian city; most of its African residents still occupy a former native enclave called the *Cité*. Until independence, downtown Kinshasa was off-limits to Africans after dark; they might as well have been in Johannesburg. The country as a whole used to have a hundred thousand permanent Belgian residents. When the Congolese began killing them off in the early 1960s, all but seventeen thousand fled. But in 1967, when the country achieved relative tranquility, they began coming back. Now there are fifty thousand Belgians in the Congo, thirty-five thousand of them in Kinshasa.

There have been changes. Kalina, the old Belgian residential area, is now integrated. Boulevard Albert is now Boulevard Trente Juin, the day of Congolese independence. King Albert's statue has been toppled, but a monument to Leopold II, who founded the colony and for a time owned the whole of it as his personal property, is still in place. For domestic political reasons, President Mobutu grumbles every so often about all the Belgians around, but he finds them useful, and they are still permitted to buy land, if they choose, and to become citizens. A lot of the Belgians in Kinshasa, for their part, grumble about the Congo nowadays, but they stay there anyway; they have longstanding financial and sentimental ties to the place, and they can earn far more money and live far more comfortably there than they could in Europe. The two groups, it is generally believed, are neatly complementary; as a former Congolese government minister once put it, Belgium and the Congo were condemned to live with each other.

Eighty times the size of Belgium, its Province Orientale alone the size of France, the Congo is hard to get around in. Before the air age, its thousands of miles of equatorial jungle constituted an effective barrier against east-west travel on the continent. For travel overland, they still do, and all the fighting of the 1960s helped to keep the Congo impenetrable. It was estimated in 1970 that it would take four hundred million dollars just to get the country's internal transportation system back to the inadequate level it was at in 1960. A couple of years ago, hoping to put some cash into the pockets of its farmers, the government exhorted them to raise more crops than they needed for their own subsistence. Quite a few farmers who responded to the call saw their excess produce rot because there was no way of moving it to a market.

Everything has moved slowly in the Congo since independence (a French dictionary not long ago rather uncharitably equated "Congolization" with "chaos"), even though the country has received more foreign aid from the United States than any other on the continent—more than half a billion dollars in the decade beginning in 1960. This largess has given the United States, and the administrators of its aid, so much power in the Congo that they sometimes seem, wittingly or unwittingly, to be running the place. Technically, the Congolese are in charge—at the top, young men mostly in their thirties, bright but uneducated, and just behind them, chafing because there is not yet really much for them to do, even younger men in their twenties, bright *and* educated. At the pinnacle, of course, is President Mobutu, a journalist before he became an army officer, who just turned forty himself in 1970. In a country torn by years of strife when he took over in 1964, his stewardship has been singularly free of rebelliousness; according to one Congolese I talked to, the principal reason is that the

Congo has simply had its fill of violence. "There is no nation on earth today that can hope to survive and at the same time permit itself the luxury of indulging in permanent revolution," my acquaintance said. "If anybody started an uprising here today, he'd probably be slaughtered by his neighbors, and we wouldn't even have to call the army out."

Just in case, though, Mobutu has a standing army of fifty thousand, with a built-in struggle for power of its own between the smooth young lieutenants who have been through the infantry course at Fort Benning, all spit-and-polish, and the only slightly older crude young colonels who have been through the jungle wars at home and still spit on the floor. The Congo is probably the only country around today with four military missions on the scene. Its air force is trained by Italy, its staff and administrative officers by Belgium, its communications and transportation officers by the United States (which also instructs the civilian police), and its paratroops by Israel. Lately, General Mobutu has been trying to play down the military origins of his authority. All his cabinet ministers are civilians, and he himself is rarely seen in uniform. Just as rarely is he seen without his special symbol of supremacy— a leopard-skin hat. To many Africans, it is the leopard, not the lion, that is truly the king of beasts (Jomo Kenyatta, too, is partial to leopard-skin headgear), and in the Congo the leopard is particularly admired. His Eminence Joseph Diangenda has an imitation leopard-skin desk blotter. The hallowed spots decorate the cover of the Congo telephone directory and the upholstery in public lounges. A leopard's head adorns the left sleeve of academic gowns, and a visiting Professor Leopard had trouble getting a painter to come to his house until he mentioned his name, upon which he was assured that his request would be accorded the highest priority.

Mobutu runs a one-party state. His Popular Republican Movement is the only party extant from among more than fifty that have sprung up since independence. The MPR is enormously powerful. After the Congo's first elections in 1970 (Mobutu won a seven-year term as president, receiving all but one hundred and fifty-seven of more than ten million votes cast), the National Assembly amended the federal Constitution to make the party the supreme authority of the land, outranking the government.

Mobutu is in some ways an enlightened autocrat. He stresses the role of women in contemporary society. He has had a woman minister in each of his cabinets, and he commands the only unit of female paratroopers in Africa. They have not yet been in combat, but they march in all the fashionable parades. They were trained by Israel. Mobutu himself took jump training there, and prominent in his army are six Israeli-trained battalions of male paratroops, one of whose principal duties is to act as a presidential bodyguard.

In 1967, the OAU held a summit conference in Kinshasa, and in discussing the various nations that were represented, among them the Arab nations of North Africa, the leading Congolese paper had some nice things to say about Israel. The Egyptians in attendance were furious and demanded that circulation of the offending issue be stopped. It was an incident indicative of the peculiar impact of the Middle East situation on black Africa. Not only are there all those Arabs along the Mediterranean coast, but there is a big Muslim presence in the black countries. Since all these nations vote not only in the OAU but also in the United Nations, Israel, in the years of African independence, has gone to great pains to solicit and cement their friendship. In a conservative capital like Kinshasa, it takes every opportunity it can find to remind the Congolese that the Arabs' friends include Communists. "Not being able to be friends with our immediate neighbors, we had to look for friends a little further off," one Israeli diplomat in Africa told me. His country has found friends as far off as South Africa, which rather admires Israel because it is vastly outnumbered by hostile neighbors supported by the Soviet Union, and which ignores the fact that Israel supports South Africa's inimical neighbors.

That support has taken many forms. Israel has set up a bee-keeping clinic in Senegal and an eye clinic in Liberia. It has helped Tanzania to start up consumer cooperatives and Uganda to plant citrus groves. It has sent poultry experts to Zambia, and cattle men to Ghana. It has built low-cost housing in Kenya and has run lotteries for a number of countries. It even sent an artist to the Ivory Coast to teach Africans how to make ceramics, using the designs they have so long carved in wood. Israel's resources are limited. Of the ten million dollars a year it allocates for foreign aid, half goes to Africa. Though by Western standards it doesn't have much in the way of funds to invest in Africa, it has people who it thinks can help the continent, and it uses them shrewdly. "We want to touch and go," an Israeli in Nairobi told me. "Jews consider knowledge preeminent, and Africans need that now more than money or industry. We've invited more than a thousand Kenyans to Israel in the last seven years, and have trained them in hotel management, in social work, in agriculture, and a lot else. Because our training is practical, when someone comes back here from Tel Aviv he can get a better job than a fellow who's had theoretical training in the same field in Britain or the States. It's nice to pass people in the street in Kenya and have them say 'Shalom!'" From the Israeli point of view, it was equally nice that from 1966 to 1970 trade between Israel and Africa increased by eighty percent.

When pro-Arab resolutions are introduced before the OAU and usually endorsed by everybody, some of the black nations urge the Israelis they know not to be upset, it's just words, it doesn't mean anything. There is reason to believe that Israel may benefit, in a roundabout way, from the excoriation heaped upon it in some of these resolutions, for a few of the black African countries are so embarrassed by what they say on the record that privately they bend over backward to be nice. (In thus behaving, of course, they exhibit political sophistication that would do credit to far more mature nations.) Whereas many countries on earth consider Africa a backwoods area and send any old emissaries there (some foreign-service men assigned to African duty wonder where they slipped up, to deserve such a fate), Israel dispatches some of its ablest emissaries to the continent, and, ignoring the barbs of the OAU, they concentrate on improving bilateral relations.

"Quite apart from our understandable desire to win over, or at least neutralize, countries that out of continental ties might tend to side with our enemies, there are a lot of reasons for our emphatic presence in Africa," another Israeli diplomat told me. "For one thing, we have a natural affinity for new, small, struggling nations, and they feel comfortable with us because, except in South Africa, we're not considered white. For another, we have demonstrated to the world that we will work with our hands—more, I'm sorry to say, than some Africans will. We are people who can come to a poor young country here and say, 'Look, your future may look as bleak as some of your landscape, but don't despair, listen to us; we know how to make a desert bloom.' For yet another, we are recognized freedom fighters. Africans talk of liberation. We won our liberation in battle. And, finally, we can sympathize with the black people wanting to Africanize their societies even if in the process a few things fall apart. We can remember the cheers at home when the first Israeli pilot took the place of a British one in an El Al cockpit. It may take Africans fifty years to do what we did in ten, but if so, so what? What if it takes a hundred? The main thing is to try to do it."

As African statesmen have found themselves, willy-nilly, caught up in the intricacies of Middle-East conflict, so have they also been involved in some of the extraterritorial skirmishing of the Far East—especially the pre-1971 battle between Peking and Taipei. While Chiang Kai-shek was struggling to retain his seat on the UN Security Council, the cornerstone of his foreign policy was to make friends with other governments and influence votes in the General Assembly. Thus, his government spent a good deal of its time buttering up the Arab nations, even though officials on Taiwan, whenever they assayed the chances of a runt taking on a giant, derived great encouragement from the feats of Israel. But Israel had only a single vote in the Assembly, whereas the ballot box was stuffed with Arabs, Taipei, accordingly, had no diplomatic relations with Tel Aviv, and it never publicly acknowledged its admiration for the only David besides North Vietnam that in modern times had humbled a Goliath. A couple of years ago, a movie about the Six-Day War reached Taiwan. A number of government officials there went to see it at a private showing and enjoyed it hugely, but it was never exhibited to the general public, for fear that the Saudi Arabian and Jordanian diplomatic missions there might take offense.

Similarly, as soon as the new independent countries emerged in Africa, Taipei and Peking began vigorously competing there in a popularity contest. Taipei won an early lead by establishing diplomatic relations with fourteen nations; the first time around,

Peking bagged only twelve. Then Chou En-lai went to Africa and gave the pendulum a hard shove; Senegal, Dahomey, and the Central African Republic swung his way. Taipei struck back. "There is an old Chinese saying, 'Till, regardless of what the harvest may bring,' and that has been our policy in Africa," one of Chiang's foreign-ministry officials told an acquaintance. To country after country, much as Israel was doing, Taipei dispatched economic and agricultural experts. A Vice-Minister of Foreign Affairs, H. K. Yang, made so many trips to Africa—twenty-two in eight years—that he became known at home as "Mr. Africa." There seemed to be heartening rewards. The tiny, remote, rice-growing village of Go-Domé, in Dahomey, held a community-wide celebration in October, 1970, in honor of Chiang's birthday. At one point, Taipei had foreign-aid missions in twenty-seven African countries, with two hundred and thirty agricultural-extension operatives in the Ivory Coast alone. President Houphouët-Boigny once complimented a Nationalist Chinese diplomat on how fit he looked. The Chinese said he kept in shape by indulging in Chinese shadow-boxing. The Ivorian murmured polite interest, and several weeks later a Chinese shadow-boxing specialist flew into Abidjan to be available at the presidential beck.

The Chinese tug of war waxed especially hot on either side of the Congo River, with Peking strongly entrenched in Brazzaville and Taipei dug in on the Kinshasa shore. One time, President Mobutu, by way of testing Taipei's efficiency, challenged a visiting Chinese Nationalist team to make something grow on a most unpromising patch of barren land. The visitors built a dam to irrigate the area, smothered it with fertilizer, and were soon producing watermelons and rice. While they were at it, the Nationalist Chinese cultivated a five-hundred-and-ninety-acre experimental farm for Mobutu at N'Sele, not far upriver from Kinshasa, and fitted it out with an ornate pagoda. (On his own, Mobutu had a swimming pool installed there that is acclaimed by the Congolese as the second largest in the world; they seem uncertain where the first is.) Mobutu became one of Chiang's staunchest African allies. When the United States ping-pong team was in Peking, turning a new page of East-West relations, the Congolese president was on a state visit to Taipei. When Peking finally triumphed at the UN, Taipei could draw some satisfaction from the fact that of the thirty-five votes it got in the General Assembly, fourteen were from Africa; but it was small comfort, and soon— in Sierra Leone, Cameroon, Ethiopia, and the other spots that climbed aboard Mao's bandwagon—Chiang's men began packing up and going home.

Not all the Asians who care about Africa have political goals. The Japanese have been much in evidence there since independence, but they haven't been soliciting votes—just business. Trade missions have arrived in planeload strength at Kinshasa. In the Katanga province of the Congo, the Japanese have a one-hundred-thousand-square-mile copper concession, and to serve it have been talking about building a thousand-mile rail line to the Atlantic Coast. A couple of hundred Japanese in the mining business have established residence down there in Lubumbashi. Of two hundred and fifty members of the Lubumbashi golf club, fifty are Japanese, and since it is difficult for many of them to converse with their fellow members, they hold their own tournaments. Other Japanese mining experts have been looking into bauxite in Ghana, iron ore in the Ivory Coast, and copper in Ethiopia. Japan is the biggest single purchaser of copper from Zambia. And Japanese products are everywhere—trucks in Uganda, locomotives in Nigeria. In Kenya, the Toyota Land Cruiser is fast replacing the British Land Rover as the standard safari vehicle; and the first man I saw anywhere in Africa wearing a pith helmet was a Japanese at the Entebbe airport in Uganda, with game-reserve patches plastered all over his bush jacket. The Japanese, like the Israelis, trade extensively with South Africa, too, but then they will trade with anybody, and the black Africans don't care what they do as long as the Sonys and Hondas keep coming along.

The Japanese, for their part, seem rather pleased with the impact they have made on the big distant continent. During some ceremonies in the Ivory Coast in observance of the tenth anniversary of its independence, a number of African women arrived wearing fancy new gowns with—as is customary throughout Africa —their president's face imprinted on them fore and aft. The Japanese ambassador whispered proudly to the United States ambassador, who not long before had been heard expressing mild satisfaction that the elevators in a new thirty-two-story government skyscraper in Abidjan were of American origin, "The fabrics were made in *our* factory."

10

The Congo—now Zaire—and Nigeria, the linchpin countries of middle Africa, contain between them nearly one-third of the black population of the continent. Both nations have survived civil wars of an intensity that almost wrecked them. Both have as presidents young army officers who got where they are by force. Though General Yakubu Gowon is a good deal less conservative than General Mobutu—in Nigerian eyes, the only legitimate Chinese government all along was that in Peking—the two heads of state have much in common. Both have sought to forestall chaos and bring some semblance of efficiency and rationality to government by a radical reshuffling of their countries' political subdivisions.

They have followed different tacks, however. Mobutu tried to achieve cohesiveness in a country long under the heel of regional despots by reducing from twenty-four to eight the number of the Congo's provinces. Gowon, hoping to prevent Nigeria's larger tribes from operating out of large political bases that could again threaten the unity of his country, raised the number of provinces from four to twelve—carving three of these out of what had been Biafra. It is indicative of the populousness of Nigeria that in just

one of the twelve postwar provinces, the Yoruba-dominated Western State, there are a dozen cities of more than one hundred thousand people, each of these thus bigger than half the capital cities
of black Africa.

Nigerians, whatever their internal conflicts, have long felt superior to other Africans. Asked one time in Addis Ababa how she
liked Ethiopia, the wife of a Nigerian diplomat stationed there
replied, rather undiplomatically, "Not at all. Very primitive country." Nigerians, at least those stationed in *their* capital, Lagos, are
very conscious of their comparative urbanity. Nothing pleases
them more than to be deferentially treated by their neighbors. It
made them proud to see how General Gowon was unarguably
Africa's man of the hour when Nigeria celebrated the tenth anniversary of *its* independence in October, 1970, just nine months
after the end of the Biafran secession. He basked happily, with
his compatriots vicariously sharing the experience, in the homage
rendered him by no less than eighteen heads of state, including Emperor Haile Selassie. The edge was somewhat taken off
the festivities by the death of Nasser, which sent many of the
distinguished guests packing off to Cairo to pay tribute to the
African man of another hour. But even so, it was a memorable
time for Gowon. He had won a long and troubling war. He had
the largest standing army on the continent—two hundred thousand strong—under his command. And now, with Nasser gone,
there seemed to be little doubt that he was the single most powerful figure in Africa. And all that at the age of thirty-six.

Soon after the end of the war, General Gowon announced that
it would probably be another six years before Nigeria would be
ready to substitute civilian for military government. He would be
only forty-two then, with plenty of time, presumably, for whatever public or private course he wished to pursue; but to some of
his fellow countrymen, languishing under a ban on political activity that went back to 1966, that seemed like rather a long while
to wait. Nonetheless, there was only little overt demurral. Nigeria
was tired of strife, and was grateful that, in Gowon, it had a
leader who came from a minor tribe and could thus be expected
to maintain a delicate balance between the three major tribes—
the Yorubas, the Ibos, and the Hausas—whose longtime wrangling

had provoked most of its internal strains. Gowon had managed, also, to attain a modus vivendi with the still powerful and semi-autonomous emirs of northern cattle-raising Nigeria. (The north, unlike the south, has no tsetse flies.) The emirs are religious potentates, too, in their largely Islam world; it is one of them whose scrutiny of the moon determines when Ramadan begins and ends. Another has a distinctive automobile horn, which his driver leans on as soon as they come within earshot of a village; this gives the inhabitants time to run out and prostrate themselves as their ruler rides past.

Gowon's chief problem at war's end was to try to pull together a never terribly united nation that was nursing the fresh wounds of fratricide. Most of his associates think he has done uncommonly well. "It was a bitter, painful war, but as soon as it ended, we outdid Lincoln," one Nigerian government official told me. "We opened our arms to each other. Enough was enough. Before the war, most of us thought in regional terms. Now reconciliation is our policy, 'One Nigeria' our motto, and nearly everybody really wants to make the nation go. No matter what any tribesman considered himself before the secession, now he wants to be a *Nigerian*. The feeling of oneness is the biggest thing around, and for that General Gowon is chiefly responsible."

While the war was on, Gowon had carefully refrained from describing the Biafrans as "enemies;" he preferred "secessionists." At the end of hostilities, he took the position that all Nigerians were once again brothers, and that the Biafrans were simply members of the family who had been temporarily misled by an aberrant brother, Odumegwu Ojukwu. There were no trials of war criminals, and relatively few detentions. Some of Ojukwu's principal associates fled Nigeria and have felt that, the government's professions of brotherhood notwithstanding, it would be imprudent for them to return. Ojukwu himself went into exile in the Ivory Coast. (In Enugu, his Biafran capital, there is a popular women's postwar coiffure, which involves winding braids of hair around the head. The style is named after Ojukwu, more or less; the Ibo term for it is roughly translatable as "He'll go around the world before he'll come back here.") But quite a few of the rebel officials are back in government jobs today. One of the three new provinces into which Biafra was divided, the East Central State, has ten commissioners, and seven of them were members of the Biafran government.

Most of the loyalists were Yorubas, and most of the rebels were Ibos. When the civil war began, one hundred and fifty Ibo students hastily departed from the University of Lagos. It had been a long-standing Yoruba tradition for its young men to indulge in facial scarification, but in the first years after independence they had stopped doing that; it had seemed an anachronism in the modern world. But when the fighting broke out, so acute were tribal antagonisms that the Yorubas had begun slashing their faces again, solely to make themselves clearly distinguishable from the hated Ibos. With feelings so intense, one would have thought that postwar reconciliation, no matter how earnestly espoused at a federal level, would have taken quite a while to achieve. But it was not so. At the end of the hostilities, the Ibos quickly returned to the University of Lagos, and soon afterward a spiritedly contested election was held there for the head of student government. There were more Yorubas enrolled than Ibos, and of the three candidates two were Yorubas and one an Ibo, and the Ibo won hands down. At about the same time, in Ibadan, the Yoruba heartland, I met a Yoruba lawyer who said he had had a nephew killed in the war, and had sworn then never again to permit an Ibo into his home, but that he, too, had been caught up in the wave of reconciliation. "I have two Ibos clerking in my office now," he said. "I have almost forgotten that there *was* a war."

The postwar visitor to Nigeria could not help wondering to what extent the surface calm cloaked inner turbulence. I asked one Ibo now employed by the federal government how he felt about the war and its aftermath, and he replied enigmatically, "A man's heart is like a woman's handbag. You never know what's inside it." Dr. Lambo, the psychiatrist who ran the University of Ibadan, and who while probing Africans' minds presumably brushed their hearts, had his own explanation for the remarkable lack of recrimination among so many of his countrymen. "There is an inherent flexibility in the African emotional structure that certainly accounts in part for our feelings of reconciliation," he told me. "This

122

stems from the African child's spending his infancy surrounded by people, so that his emotions are diffused rather than concentrated. He is touched by everybody's hands and carried on a dozen backs. He never suffers from isolation, and his emotions are lightly structured. When he grows up, all this expresses itself in a number of ways. Now, in the Western world, you have the phenomenon of grief so deep it can drive people to suicide. Here, when someone dies, you may have an upsurge of great emotional excitement, but it doesn't last. At an African funeral, people sob and faint and beat their heads against the ground, but a day later, if not half an hour later, it is all in the past and they are laughing. This is not surmise, but a clinical observation. And so it is here with individual violence. A man may go into a frenzy and chop another man to death with a machete, but then he is apt to sit down quietly and wait for the police to come and get him. And a group of men may battle each other savagely in a war, as our people did, but when the war ends that is that and they quietly go back about their business."

One of the strangest postscripts to the civil war has been the universal lack of knowledge about the casualties that resulted from it. Certainly people were killed and wounded; the Lagos government has a project under way to train specialists in the manufacture and fitting of artificial limbs. Yet when it comes to body counts, bewilderment sets in. "Never before in history was there a war in which so much ammunition was shot and so few lives lost," a knowledgeable non-Nigerian in Lagos told me. Before the war ended, the outside world had been told many a time that two million Nigerians, mostly on the Biafran side, had perished. Ojukwu has asserted the figure could be even higher; Gowon, for his part, has said two hundred thousand would be closer to the truth. But just as in the spirit of brotherliness he has frowned on medals or monuments to commemorate the fratricide, so he has seemingly discouraged the collection of reliable statistics. More than a year after the last shot was fired, his own Ministry of Information was insisting it had no idea of the actual casualties incurred by either side. "My guess is that not only does the government not know how many casualties there were but that it doesn't

know how many people it had in the army," an American diplomat in Lagos told me. "It seems hard to believe that two million
people could have been killed, but it probably doesn't matter
much one way or the other, because that's the number that has
become fixed in people's minds. Our government has used that
figure, but there's no evidence that we had any source for it other
than the newspapers, or that the papers had any source other than
Biafran propaganda. Take what happened with the 1967 massacres
in the north of the country. The Biafrans claimed at the time that
five thousand Ibos were killed there, and we at the Embassy
tended to think that was probably correct. But then as time went
on the figure began to grow, and it kept on growing, and without
anybody else's having been killed it finally got up to thirty thousand, and that sort of became the historical figure, and it's easier
to go along with it than suggest that it just doesn't make sense."

At one point, after the war, the American Embassy tried to
make its own unofficial enumeration of war casualties. It went
about this by having its staff ask every Ibo they ran into how
many friends or relatives of his had died. Very few of those ques-
tioned knew of anybody. When after the war the schools in what
had been Biafra reopened, nearly all the children who'd been in
them before the war came back. There were ten thousand policemen in Nigeria before the war, more than half of them Ibos;
according to the federal Ministry of Information, only four members
bers of the force died in combat. One of Nigeria's most respected
civil servants, Allison Ayida, who is now permanent secretary in
the Ministry of Finance, told me, "I personally didn't lose a single
friend in the war."

And what of the starving Biafran children whose pictures the
world saw and lamented? Surely some of *them* died. Yes, of
course, the war in Biafra was an infantry war, and as ground troops
move back and forth in any war, children in their path get hurt.
There had never been enough food in Biafra in peacetime, moreover, to sustain its inhabitants; that was one reason why more than
a million Ibos had moved to other parts of the country. But were
the pictures real or faked? One can greet with skepticism the suggestion by the Lagos government that the familiar photographs

may not have been taken in Biafra at all, but in the Congo, and were distributed with new captions by a Swiss public relations firm retained by the Biafrans. But what does one make of the assertion by Clyde Ferguson, the neutral American envoy who tried to get relief supplies into Biafra, that he *knows* the pictures were taken in the Congo?

In the spirit of reconciliation, the Lagos government announced immediately after the war that it was allocating some twenty-five million dollars for the rehabilitation of essential services in the secessionist area. The money was slow, though, in forthcoming. The Lagos government declared on June 30, 1970, that a state of emergency it had decreed in the Biafran area was over, but not for quite a while after that did it fully open up the airport at Enugu, the principal city of the region. Nor did it seem over-anxious to restore television service to the losers in the war. When a Ministry of Information man was asked when this was apt to come about, he shrugged and said, "It's not one of the priorities." Some Ibos think they have in such persnickety ways been punished for their intransigence. Many of them are living through their own particular version of reconciliation: They are reconciled to being losers and to having to make the best of that role. And in case they entertain any further notions of rebellion, the federal government keeps a large military garrison around.

Not a few Ibos took it as further punitive affront that during the tenth-anniversary celebration in Lagos, the federal government commandeered for a press center the home of Sir Louis Ojukwu, the father of their defeated leader; they were not impressed by the government's straightfaced statement that that particular house had been selected by chance. By and large, however, the Ibos came out of the war feeling quite chipper, considering what they had been through. They had always been the technicians and professionals of Nigeria, but before the war they had had the reputation, like Jews, of being clever, ambitious, assertive—and unmanly. Now, even in defeat, they could compare themselves to those Middle-East Jews who had also been considered timid—until they showed the Arabs otherwise. (During the civil war in Nigeria, Israel officially sided with the federal government, but its support was restrained, and many Israelis—conceivably stirred by reports that the Lagos government had genocidal intentions toward the Biafrans—sympathized with the eventual losers.)

However the defeated Ibos might feel about themselves, there remained in Nigeria ingrained anti-Iboists who were in no forgive-and-forget mood. Port Harcourt, now the capital of the newly created Rivers State, was before the war inhabited mainly by the Ijaw tribe, but its commercial life was dominated by Ibos. One enterprise they didn't own was the British-controlled Kingsway chain of department stores. Because the British were backing the federal government during the war, and because the convenience of Ijaws mattered little to the Biafrans, they burned down the Kingsway store in Port Harcourt, though they left alone the one in Enugu. So at the end of the war Enugu had its Kingsway and Port Harcourt did not, and the permanent residents of the latter city reacted coolly to General Gowon's plea to bury the hatchet. The story is told of one Ibo who returned to his former place of work in Port Harcourt and, while a government bureaucrat looked on beamingly, was received with a great show of warmth by his fellow workers. But as soon as the visitors were out of earshot, the workers rushed into their boss's office and said, "You're not going to hire *that* guy back, are you?" Outside of Port Harcourt, however, most Ibos are now back in their old jobs, or in new and better ones. Many of them shrug off the war today as if it had been a trifling domestic spat. One of the country's principal lawyers declared, while the war was on, that he would rather be dead than ever again live under the federal government; now, very much back in that establishment, he conducts a lucrative law practice in Lagos.

As a more or less reunified nation, Nigeria came out of its internal ordeal in fairly good economic shape. The war had cost the central government seven hundred and fifty million dollars to prosecute—just a couple of days' running expenses for an American war but a whopping outlay for Africa—and yet Lagos had financed it on a cash basis, paying for the arms it got from Britain and Russia practically on delivery, and as a result ending up unsaddled by war debts. To conserve its foreign exchange, the country had sharply curtailed its imports; instead of exporting the cotton it grew to mills in England, for instance, as had long been the practice, Nigeria had built a mill of its own. Since the Lagos government had received few outright gifts from the outside world, it did not feel beholden to anyone. On an official level, America took no sides during the war; privately, most Americans who paid any attention at all to it sympathized with, and supported, the underdog Biafrans. Right at the end of the war, the United States flew in twenty-one plane loads of emergency relief supplies. To make the gift palatable to the federal officials who would be distributing it, it was delivered on air force planes with all identifying markings painted over, and the crews that manned them were given a special uniform allowance for the mercy mission, to buy civilian shirts and slacks to wear instead of their possibly provocative uniforms.

The Nigerians have mellowed, but many of them still regard Americans with distrust. The first Nigerian government man I spoke to was an immigration official at the Dahomeyan border who, after ascertaining that I was a reporter, said "Welcome to Nigeria, but only if you write good things about it." Later, on a higher level, at the foreign office in Lagos, a member of the secretariat said, "Nigeria is as truly nonaligned as a country can be today, because we learned during the war that in international relations there are no such things as traditional friends. We've heard Americans complain in recent months that we don't seem to fall all over ourselves being hospitable to them. Well, the simple fact is that we have reason to suspect that quite a few Americans are still pro-Biafran and think the war is still on and that Ibos are still dying, and how can we be sure that when Americans who feel like that get over here they won't try to stir things up? Anyone who comes here to help *all* Nigerians and not just one section of our people will be welcome. But we're apprehensive about foreigners who want to come and refight wars that have already been won and forgiven."

Not entirely forgiven. About three hundred Nigerians live in Zambia, and all of them were invited to a party in Lusaka to celebrate the tenth anniversary of their homeland's independence.

Reconciliation was the motif of the event. Most of the Hausa traders who sell art objects in the shops along Cairo Road turned up, wearing their turbans and flowing white robes, but most of the Ibos boycotted the affair. The most embattled individuals around appeared to be the resident American black women who had Nigerian husbands. Those married to Ibos, a year after the war was over, were still not on speaking terms with the wives of Yorubas.

11

Some Nigerians believe today that their civil war was largely waged because of the offshore oil with which their land has proved to be richly endowed. Some of the oil is within the boundaries of what was Biafra. An Anglo-Dutch consortium had a concession from the Lagos government to exploit most of the oil, and there was reason to believe that a permanently independent Biafra would have dealt instead with French and Portuguese interests. It seems indisputable that France and Portugal—not to mention South Africa—find it easier to exert what pressure they can still bring to bear in Africa on small nations than on large ones; they would probably have been just as happy to see Nigeria broken up not merely into two countries but a dozen. African oil is a prize worth jousting for. There have been oil strikes up and down much of the West African coast. Big countries like the Congo have been meditating with interest about the economic good fortune of places like Saudi Arabia, and little countries like Dahomey about that of Kuwait.

So far, Nigeria has got the jump on all of the continent. Nigeria has known crude-oil reserves of two hundred million tons, probable reserves of six hundred million tons, and possible reserves of twelve hundred million tons. The big combination of Royal Dutch-Shell and British Petroleum began production in a small way in 1958, and by 1966, just before the civil war began, was producing five hundred and seventy thousand barrels a day. Since the end of the war, the total output for all the companies operating in Nigeria has reached over a million and a half barrels daily, and the cornerstone of the country's postwar economy has been its oil royalties—about seventy-five cents a barrel, or three hundred million dollars, annually. Lagos has become a boom town. Twenty-five American oil-drilling and oil-equipment companies are on the scene, and there is a severe shortage of housing that meets Western standards. Some oil men have paid five years' stiff rent in advance to obtain suitable accommodations.

Nigeria attracts relatively few tourists: in 1970, it issued five hundred visas a month to Americans for all purposes; over the same stretch, nearly three times that number of Americans visited the United States ambassador to Kenya in a single month. Nonetheless, the big Federal Palace Hotel in Lagos is now frequently booked solid. It is owned by the government, which during the war, when there were few visitors of any sort, tried to persuade several foreign hotel chains to take it over. Nobody was interested, so the government ran the place itself, and it has proved to be another tidy source of income. With that management, moreover, the Federal Palace can provide entertainment that might have been difficult to book under civilian auspices: the Police Band plays in the main bar on Saturday nights.

Petroleum is so much on Nigerian minds these days that in a national development plan covering the years between 1970 and 1974 the whole economy was divided into just two sectors—oil and non-oil. In those four years, Nigeria expects its non-oil foreign trade to show a deficit of around three billion dollars, but oil income should offset all but a few hundred million of this. And petroleum is only one of its largely untapped resources. Nigeria has coal, tin, bauxite, lead, iron, zinc, and—let the South Africans think about *that!*—even a little gold. But Nigerians have no intention of giving outside investors free-wheeling rein to profit from their potential wealth. The government has restrictions on profit-taking that would make a colonialist wince. "Of course there will

130

be profits for everybody from our oil," a government man in Lagos told me, "but at the same time we have pretty severe tax laws. We see foreign investment in Nigeria not as a chance for someone to get rich off us but as a cooperative effort to help us in our development. And if people don't want to play the game according to our rules, that's their business. We're not begging for investment. From now on, we're not begging from anybody for anything."

Oil notwithstanding, Nigeria, like most of black Africa, is still a predominantly agricultural nation. Seventy percent of all Nigerians are in the agricultural labor force—eighty percent if one counts fishing, animal husbandry, and forestry. As Nigeria is rich in minerals, so does it have just about all the cash crops that Africa relies on: timber, rubber, cocoa, coffee, peanuts, and palm oil. And, unlike some of its neighboring countries, most of Nigeria's land is arable. Still, much of this is at the moment only marginally productive. Across the continent, for three or four hundred miles both north and south of the Equator, a good deal of the earth is a reddish soil called laterite, which is better suited to road- and house-building than to planting. And it has never been well used. Africans will exhaust the productivity of one patch of land and then abandon it and move on to another. The upshot has been that Africa barely manages to grow enough food to meet its needs, and as its population increases, so do its needs.

For nearly a decade, this situation has been a matter of concern to the Rockefeller and Ford Foundations, which, marching side by side in the Green Revolution, have jointly created the International Rice Research Institute in the Philippines and the International Maize and Wheat Improvement Center in Mexico. Now, in Ibadan, they are putting the final touches on another philanthropic venture, the International Institute of Tropical Agriculture. It will concentrate on research in food crops rather than export crops—roots like cassavas and yams, cereals like rice and maize, grain legumes like cowpeas and soybeans. At full strength, the Institute will be manned by thirty-odd resident scientists—plant pathologists, nematologists, entomologists, and so on —from a dozen countries. The director is Dr. Herbert R. Albrecht,

131

a plant breeder and geneticist who was president of North Dakota State University. Ibadan was chosen as the site because the university already there had an excellent agricultural faculty, and because the Nigerian government gave the Institute twenty-two hundred acres. When finished, the Institute—boasting its own two-hundred-acre artificial lake, eight and a half miles of chain-link fence (to discourage cattle-grazers and pilferers), and a bilingual library (to encourage francophone agriculturists to share in its eventual findings)—will represent an outlay on the part of its two sponsors of seventeen and a half million dollars. It may also eventually keep Africa from starving.

The new Institute also has the best roads anywhere in Nigeria, made not of laterite but of asphalt. Most of Nigeria's roads got badly chewed up during the war, and to rehabilitate them is a high government priority—higher, apparently, a few still dissident Ibos have muttered, than the rehabilitation of undernourished children afflicted with kwashiorkor. Driving in Nigeria can be a perilous adventure. "Safe journey" is a traditional bon-voyage greeting, and it is said with heartfelt meaning. From a feature story in the Lagos *Daily Times,* under the headline "How To Stay Alive on Nigerian Roads," one could deduce that the chief medical concern of the country—and this at a time when a cholera epidemic was bearing down on it like a truck without brakes—was that, because of a rash of auto accidents, there were no more beds available in Lagos' orthopedic hospital. In anglophone Nigeria, traffic moves to the left. In 1972, it is scheduled to shift to the right, but the joke in Lagos is that it won't make any discernible difference because all Nigerians drive in the middle of the road anyway.

Particularly carefree are the drivers of the decrepit, overcrowded, low-fare passenger buses called mammy wagons, each with its own name—"Beware," "God First," "In the Name of Allah," "John Wayne," "Still Alive," and the like. The mammy wagons bounce off each other, or off passing trucks, with disconcerting regularity. After a crash, it is the fraternal custom for bystanders to wander around passing their hats for tow-truck expenses or funeral expenses, depending on the circumstances. Along Nigeria's busiest thoroughfare, the eighty-two-mile, largely two-lane stretch between Lagos and Ibadan, I once counted twenty-seven wrecks. Merely one of these, a dreadful mess involving an oil truck, a cattle lorry, a mammy wagon, and, underneath it all, a crumpled Volkswagen, held me up for an hour. While I was hanging around waiting for the debris to be cleared away, a Nigerian who was taking up a collection—the more serious kind—called my attention to the name of the mammy wagon involved: "Safe Journey."

In Lagos one day, I met a man who had started up a successful business. He owned a fleet of long-haul trucks that had closed bodies and lockable doors. He said he was doing very nicely even though he had to pay his drivers high deterrent wages, to keep their cargos intact. If crime is a worldwide problem, then Nigeria could be said to be sitting on top of the world. The motorist traveling after dark is apt to be flagged down every couple of miles by armed men in uniform. Ostensibly, they are supposed to be deterrents themselves, against highway robbery, but their pay is low and now and then they forget which side of the law they are on. It is also difficult in Nigeria, these days, to tell a genuine soldier from a deserter. Suffice to say that most Nigerian provinces, in further espousal of deterrence, now consider armed robbery a capital offense. Executions for that crime have lately averaged about six a month. When the Midwestern State not long ago put four convicted robbers up before a firing squad, it did so in a stadium. A capacity crowd of twenty-seven thousand looked on. In Lagos, a similar event attracted one hundred and sixty-five thousand gawkers.

Inasmuch as there are more soldiers in the ex-Biafran East Central State than in any other, there is more crime, some of it with Robin-Hoodish overtones. One highway patrol, stopping a truck that turned out to have six bootleggers in it, forced the rascals to drink their own gin until they collapsed, and, leaving them half-dead at the roadside, drove off in their vehicle. There is scarcely an urban home in Nigeria of any prosperity that does not have its own night watchman; these sentries constitute so large a consumer market that the sellers of Sony transistor radios address advertisements specifically to them. Two expatriates' homes I visited in Africa were further guarded by German shepherds trained, their masters said, to bite black people. This enhanced security but was hard on the household help, who occasionally got nipped while going about their duties.

The most worrisome crimes in Nigeria, though, as in much of black Africa, do not involve violence but, rather, corruption. The exchange of bribes—"dash" is the common African term—is so closely woven into the fabric of African life that many Nigerians, while conceding that General Gowon is praiseworthily incorruptible himself, at the same time speculate that the gravest threat to his regime is his inability to keep his subordinates in line. His government has plastered the nation with posters advocating upright behavior. One shows a businessman kissing his secretary in his office. "No!—Not Here," the caption cries. But such injunctions are not always heeded. At the Lagos airport, two uniformed customs men on duty blandly extracted some dash from me within a few feet of a sign declaring that customs men are forbidden to accept money for any reason unless they give a signed receipt. All I got was a crooked grin. On another visit to the same airport, however, a Nigerian Air Force officer took it upon himself to save me from a fleecing at the hands of a taxi driver. The officer ordered the driver to charge me less than a fee that—in my anxiety to get out of there fast—I had already agreed on. The driver was furious, but he didn't argue with the officer. There are times when one almost gives thanks for military governments. On that occasion, I expressed mine by giving the officer three dollars' dash. I had given Nigerians a good deal more for doing a good deal less.

12

The coup d'état has become an old institution in new Africa. In the 1960s, there were a score of uprisings against the governments of the independent black nations on the continent. It was not altogether surprising. Practically all these countries had been going through a period of political flux, and, being largely one-party states, they had no built-in constitutional means for changing governments other than by force. Of all the countries that have undergone this abrupt shift in authority, only two—Ghana and Upper Volta—had by the middle of 1971 reverted to civilian rule. And at that one-third of the fifty-seven members of the Upper Voltan parliament were required by law to be army officers. Ghana, for its part, had attributed its singularity to plain good fortune. "Not many countries in the world," a government pamphlet there declared, "can boast of a luck, such as Ghana's, in returning to civilian government so soon after a military coup."

The African coups, by and large, have been comparatively blood-less, but the mere prospect of being caught up in one of them can make foreigners edgy. When I was in Senegal, the sight of some policemen at the main post office prompted a Frenchman to wonder if a coup was in the making, when in fact the police were merely rerouting traffic while a street was being widened. When I flew to Liberia the next day, an Englishman seated alongside me, on learning that our landing would be delayed, wondered if troops had taken over the airport; the reason turned out to be ground fog. Most of the natives are not so restless. During the Ghana coup that deposed Kwame Nkrumah in 1966, when Accra was momentarily paralyzed, a concerned American asked his African driver how he would feed his family, and the African shrugged and said he guessed he would hop a bus up to his uncle's place in the country and get himself a bag of yams. Africans, above all, are unembarrassed by the volatility of their governments; the present president of Togo admits to having personally assassinated his predecessor. In countries as far apart ideologically and geographically as Tanzania and Liberia, I was told by African officials that most of the people on the continent regard coups d'état as part of the normal process of national growth.

Until early in 1971, however, the coup had been largely a *West* African phenomenon—if one may properly use "phenomenon" to describe something so commonplace. True, there had been a few near misses in East Africa, and some nervousness, particularly among those who stood to lose the most—their jobs—from an overthrow. (How quickly the apprehension in the voice of an employee of the Zambian Ministry of Information turned to relief when he was told, on inquiring from air traffic control about a worrisome object he'd just sighted in the sky, that it was merely a research balloon launched by the university!) The government of Tanzania, which survived an abortive coup in 1964, subsequently banned from public sale a book entitled *Coup d'Etat*. In Ethiopia, early in 1971, while Emperor Haile Selassie was in his fifty-fifth year of a reign that obviously couldn't last forever, a government official told me that when His Imperial Majesty passed on there was unlikely to be a military takeover because—it hardly sounded like an orderly reason—there were only sixty thousand men in the army whereas in Addis Ababa alone there were more than one hundred thousand rifles and machine guns in the hands of civilians. "Every friend I have here has a machine gun, and I have one, too," he said. The stability of Ethiopia has been in no small part dependent, for the past decade, on American military support, but the government man had a large portrait of Mao Tse-Tung on the inside of his office door. "If the Americans pull out, I might as well be prepared," he said. Even in Kenya, perhaps the most tranquil of all spots in East Africa—at least while Jomo Kenyatta remained at its helm—an African doctor I gave a lift to one day remarked apropos of nothing at all that he was prepared to take up arms. Against whom, I asked. "I don't know," he said. "You never know."

The coup came suddenly and swiftly to East Africa early in the morning of January 25, 1971, when President Apolo Milton Obote of Uganda was overthrown by Major General Idi Amin, the Chief of Staff of his army. In retrospect, there were those who professed to be not in the least surprised. Hindsight aside, though, Obote had, in African terms, seemed relatively secure. He himself had said nearly five years earlier that while other anglophone nations like Ghana and Nigeria apparently had to endure coups to achieve stability, he had every reason to believe he could avoid one. And as recently as August, 1970, he had had a tract printed reasserting an earlier self-assessment as "perhaps the only African leader not afraid of a military takeover." Perhaps he relied too heavily on a reputation he had earned of being one of Africa's preeminent conciliators; statesmen who hung around British Commonwealth circles had taken to calling him "a black Menzies."

Only four days before Obote's downfall, all had seemed so surface-quiet in his capital, Kampala—a pleasant city of three hundred and forty thousand with a mild Asian flavor—that the Kampala correspondent of the *Daily Nation,* in Nairobi, had found nothing more trenchant to file than a jocose recipe for a Uganda Tea Cocktail. (East Africa produces eighty-five million pounds of tea a year, the bulk of it from Uganda, whose lush plantations are a visual delight. The recipe called for three jiggers of cold tea, a dash of lime juice, and two jiggers of *waragi,* a banana-based Ugandan gin. This last ingredient made the item sort of newsworthy, because Kenya, which was supposed to have close economic links to Uganda, had not long before prohibited the importation of *waragi.* Kenyans, the *Daily Nation* writer said, could substitute ordinary gin.) I had been in Uganda myself only three weeks before the coup, principally to visit Murchison Falls and the Albert Nile, teeming with crocodiles and hippopotamuses and perch so fat that fishermen are enjoined to throw back any they catch under twenty-five pounds. (Leaving Murchison Falls National Park, I had stopped at a roadside marker that testified to the African awareness of the interrelationship of man and beast; it had been erected in memory of a chap who had been crushed to death between two elephants while sitting at that spot beneath a palm tree.) In Kampala, which has few animals outside of a bat sanctuary, none of the government people I spoke to even hinted at the expectation of anything untoward. The United States Ambassador was about to take off on a skiing holiday in Switzerland.

Kampala has two principal men's social centers, the Kampala Club and the Uganda Club. Both are officially integrated, but the older, the Kampala Club, is still largely frequented by whites. Back in the 1950s, the British Governor General of Uganda, the late Sir Andrew Cohen, tried to get the expatriates' clubs in town to admit Africans. He was an enlightened colonial administrator. He put through laws giving Africans a financial interest in cotton-ginning and coffee-processing, and allowing them to drink whiskey. But he couldn't persuade the clubs to change their non-black membership policies, so with government funds he started the multiracial Uganda Club. He was soon eased out of Africa.

The Uganda Club has only a handful of white members. Most Ugandans high in the government go there daily. I was taken there early one afternoon by a Ugandan with highly placed connections who within a few minutes introduced me to two cabinet ministers who were relaxing in the lounge. The minister of defense bought me a *waragi*-and-tonic, and while we were sipping and chatting somebody came along and told him the cabinet was meeting. "Oh, I suppose I should be there," he said. Instead, he beckoned a waiter to bring us the other half, and he told me that when some government officials heard that the president was about to drop in at the club—which he did almost every evening—they would hastily duck out, because Obote would like as not keep them up all night talking. At five o'clock one morning, it seemed, one minister had felt bold enough to blurt out that the wives of all the men in the president's captive audience of that moment would shortly be giving them a hard time, because how could you expect a woman to believe a husband's explanation that he had stayed out all night palavering with the president? Obote had at once instructed his security guards to take down the names of all those present, telephone their homes, and invite their wives to join him and them for breakfast at the club an hour later.

In 1966, when he was prime minister, Obote had engineered the exile of the first president of Uganda, Sir Edward Mutesa II, who was also the King of Buganda. Known as King Freddie, he held the title of Kabaka, and was highly esteemed by his tribe of two million, the Baganda. Sir Edward became an alcoholic drifter in London and died there, impoverished, in the fall of 1969. That Obote had got away with this move was a tribute to his power, for the Kings of Buganda were a powerful lot themselves. Before independence, the British technically had a protectorate over all of Uganda, but inasmuch as Kampala was the capital of the King of Buganda, the British prudently established their administrative headquarters at Entebbe, with a deputy in Kampala who was a *de facto* ambassador to the Kabaka. Even after independence, there had been a Bugandan Parliament in Kampala, while the supposedly superior federal parliament operated out of Entebbe.

President Obote, like President Nyerere in Tanzania and President Kaunda in Zambia, had long had socialistic leanings. On Obote's initiative, Uganda had, in April of 1965, become the first non-Communist nation to denounce American intervention in Vietnam. It had sometimes seemed hard to tell, though, whether Obote's particular brand of socialism—there are several variations on the continent—was sincere or opportunistic. And in any event, "socialism" is not a bugaboo word in Uganda, or, when it comes to that, in much of black Africa. "Look, Africans are born socialists," the minister of defense said to me at the Uganda Club. "There's no two ways about it. I may own two hundred head of cattle, but do they really belong to me? Of course not. They belong to my clan. 'Socialism' is merely a reaffirmation of what we've been doing for generations, and when you get right down to it, it isn't much different from what you're doing in America—free education, free medical service, free roads and communications, help for the farmers, and so on. The only real difference is that we don't tolerate the exploitation of men by men."

Obote was not universally beloved. On December 19, 1969, a would-be assassin shot him in the cheek. ("I had a bad accident" was his only public comment on the incident.) Almost immediately afterward, he announced a "Common Man's Charter" for Uganda, a program whereby the country would move, in all areas, to the left—would get away, among other things, from what he called "the domain of the Mercedes Benz," which for so many Africans was, and still is, a special status symbol. Obote's proposals were not notably different from those Nyerere and Kaunda had put forth, but he *called* his scheme a "Move to the Left," and the words had a scary sound to outsiders. One of the sinistral steps he took was, in the spring of 1970, to nationalize eighty-four companies largely owned by expatriates—tea plantations, industries, banks, insurance companies, and so on. Uganda, in 1969, had enjoyed an eleven-percent growth in its gross national product, but not much of this had benefited any Ugandans; just about all the profits went straight to England. The British accepted the new order of things with characteristic imperturbability; the reaction of the chairman of the National and Grindlay's Bank to the usurpation of sixty percent of its shares (at a price determined by the Ugandan government) was to present Obote with a silver cigarette box. When Amin supplanted Obote, he decreed that in three-quarters of the cases of nationalized companies the government would take only a forty-nine percent interest. Presumably Obote got to keep the cigarette box. After the coup, it was just about all he had left.

In January, 1971, Prime Minister Heath of England convened a summit conference of the Commonwealth countries at Singapore. The main issue on the agenda—the main one to the black Commonwealth nations, if not to Heath—was the proposed sale of arms by Britain to South Africa. It was so touchy a subject that when, that same month, the Association of Commonwealth Literature and Language Studies had its triennial meeting in Jamaica, the participants resolved at the outset not even to mention the concurrent meeting at Singapore; once the matter was raised, they feared, they'd never get around to discussing any academic affairs. Back in Uganda, Obote said flatly that if Britain helped South Africa, Uganda would secede from the Commonwealth. But Nyerere, who had long been Obote's mentor—and who was to give him refuge after the coup—had been more circumspect. He was just as strongly opposed to any sale of arms, but to him the Commonwealth had been an invaluable multiracial institution, one of the few, in a world torn every which way between black and white, rich and poor, strong and weak, left and right, that seemed worth clinging to.

There is an understandable reluctance among African leaders with worries at home to travel afield. They remember too well how Nkrumah was ousted while in Asia. Obote had declined previously to leave Uganda. But he was determined to speak out in Singapore, and so he went there, although no one knew better than he that he had internal problems, most of them involving his army and General Amin. Obote came from the Lango tribe, and the Langos and the Acholis, both prominent in military circles, had long been on the outs with General Amin, a West Nile tribesman. Moreover, Obote was concerned about the General's getting himself mixed up in religious politics. There were two principal Islamic groups in Uganda: the National Association for the Advancement of Muslims, founded by a Lango who was President Obote's cousin, and the Uganda Muslim Community, which consisted mainly of Bagandans and whose leader Obote had seen fit to imprison. Amin, like Obote, had always been partial to the NAAM, but lately he had been seen at meetings of the UMC, and the president didn't much fancy that. The two men had had a stormy confrontation, and as an upshot of their growing differences Obote tried to diminish Amin's strength by promoting a few dozen other officers and entangling his chain of command.

By the time Obote left for Singapore, there appears to have been no doubt in either protagonist's mind that the country was not big enough for both of them. Obote almost certainly planned to get rid of Amin when he returned home. So Amin struck first. He justified his action by a bill of complaints conveniently drawn up by some of his soldiers. It was a somewhat surrealistic document: it accused Obote of, among other laxities, having acquired ten palaces, and of overindulgence in wine, women, and even smoking. The seventeenth of eighteen points the soldiers made—rather curious, on the eve of a coup—went, "The Army has always tried to be an example to the whole of Africa by not taking over the government." It was as if the writers of the document believed that the taking over of governments was somehow a routine function of African armies. The motto of independent Uganda is "For God and our country." President Obote had rarely neglected to include the phrase in his pronouncements, and now the soldiers concluded with "We have done this for God and our country." By the time Obote could scramble back from Asia to Africa, he had no country to return to. Frustratedly staying in Tanzania, he would learn a few months later that Amin would pay a reward of $139,200 to any one who produced him in Uganda, alive. In a part of Africa long on professional hunters but short on cash, it was a tempting offer.

I happened still to be in East Africa at the time of the coup, and, curious to visit a country that had just been through the experience, I returned to Uganda on one of the first planes allowed back in. At the Entebbe airport, the souvenir shop and bar were locked up, but some soldiers lounging around the waiting room were plentifully supplied with beer. Inasmuch as while swigging it they were also toying with guns and bullets, they invited deference.

There had been some damage to the airport. Just a few hours after the coup, a Sabena airliner flew in from Kigali, in Rwanda. When the pilot asked over his radio for landing instructions, the control tower waved him off, but the pilot, not knowing anything about a coup and being short of fuel, came in anyway. As he was taxiing toward the terminal, some soldiers opened fire, and, fuel or no fuel, he gunned his engines and took off again, undamaged. Out of pique, a tank then fired a shell at the main entrance, killing two European priests, and there had been further small-arms fire, for no discernible reason, within the terminal; it was clear from the bullet holes that the gents' room had been a special target. But at my arrival, five days after the derring-do, the front entrance was already under repair, and Entebbe itself looked as tranquil as I remembered it; in the heat of forenoon, the only sign of activity was furnished by two men rolling a tennis court at the Entebbe Club. Many of the trucks on the highway to Kampala had tree branches on top of them—a symbol of celebration of deliverance from tyranny, my driver told me—and some truck drivers had large photographs of General Amin interposed between themselves and their windshields—a dubious incentive to safety, I didn't have to be told, in a nation that already ranked second only to Nigeria in its road-accident rate.

Along the twenty-five-mile stretch to the capital, I saw only two military vehicles, jeeps with machine guns mounted on them; and these were offset by two zebra-striped Volkswagen minibuses with tourists mounted in them. Kampala hardly looked as though it had been through a revolution. A few people were pointedly dressed in blue and white, the royal colors of the Kings of Buganda, whose followers were especially pleased with the turn of events. (One of Amin's early actions as Uganda's new president was to bring King Freddie's body back from London for ceremonial interment; two hundred thousand Ugandans filed past the corpse.) I headed for the seventeen-story Apolo Hotel, on a hill in the middle of the city. It rises above a potentially even grander structure, which Obote had been building to accommodate a summit conference of the Organization of African Unity scheduled for July, 1971. The new edifice had been budgeted at sixteen million dollars (the annual federal budget for the whole country was only one hundred and six million), and under Obote construction had gone on practically around the clock—even on Christmas day. Now, work was continuing, though it seemed improbable that the OAU would meet in a country whose new president few of its members were apt to recognize soon, if ever. The OAU conference was ultimately held in Addis Ababa and was boycotted by a number of countries, including Amin's Uganda.

Work *had* halted on another Obote monument, a new headquarters building for his political party, the United Peoples' Congress. The Apolo Hotel—formally known by Obote's first name and informally, because of his middle name, as the "Milton Hilton"—had three hundred rooms, but since it opened in 1967 it had been filled only once. That was when Pope Paul VI visited Kampala in July, 1970—the first trip by any Pontiff to any part of Africa. It was a splashy occasion. A local soft-drink bottler put up a sign saying "Pepsi Welcomes the Pope," and many Africans who would ordinarily wear shirts with their national leader's portrait on them had decked themselves out in shirts jointly featuring the Pope and the President. As soon as the coup began, Obote's portrait, thitherto on view in practically every building in the country, down to the tiniest street stall, came into disrepute; a principal sound effect of any African coup is the tinkling of smashed picture-frame glass. Amin at first declined to let his new subjects tear down a large bronze medallion of Obote that ornamented the entrance of the Parliament building in Kampala; in fact, the General said that he was keeping his own autographed photo of Obote at home, inasmuch as it was an authentic part of Ugandan history. (The prudent headmaster of an Asian school, when his pupils demanded that he take down Obote's picture, compromised by turning it to the wall and putting Amin's on the other side; whatever quirky way destiny might move, he wanted to be ready to move with it.) Amin, souring on his victim and taking his chances with history, subsequently let the medallion be pried off the Parliament building; one wonders what happened to all the Papal shirts. Now, the Apolo Hotel was nearly empty. There were a few journalists on hand, a few tourists who'd been trapped by the coup, and a pair of European beer salesmen making their regular rounds of their territory. Aside from its dearth of patrons, the hotel was running smoothly. None of the guests, though, seemed to be putting out their shoes at night. Maybe they wanted to keep them handy.

Coups are violent, but in a way they are less convulsive than more theoretically orderly changes of government—Democratic to Republican, Conservative to Labor, or whatever. Coups are cheaper, quicker, and less acrimonious, and they do not always produce appreciably more casualties. In the Amin coup, probably not more than one hundred people died. There was little visible damage in Kampala. The approaches to a few gas stations had been chewed up by armored-car treads. (It is a rare African driver of any kind of vehicle, be it tank or taxi, who fills up with fuel before embarking on a mission.) There was a curfew on—from 7 P.M. to 6:30 A.M. (one newspaper in Kenya could not resist saying that Ugandan wives were overjoyed, because their husbands would for once have to spend their evenings at home)—and when I went around to the central police station to get an after-hours pass I noticed that a tank had knocked down part of a retaining wall there. But security was amazingly light. I walked freely into and through the police station; it is something one can't do in New York nowadays. There was some desultory shooting that night—probably just soldiers testing their weapons out of curiosity —but for the most part life in Kampala had already returned to normal, albeit at the regrettably necessary postponement of the annual general meeting of the Uganda Association of Women's Organizations.

Nowhere was the lack of tight security more evident than at General Amin's two-story stucco house on Prince Charles Drive, which he was then also using as an office. I wandered over there on a day when Obote, in Dar es Salaam, was vowing to return by whatever means necessary (the *Daily Nation* in Nairobi, now thoroughly covering Kampala, observed dryly that "Obote's threatening behavior is reminiscent of Dr. Nkrumah's when he sought refuge in Guinea, becoming co-President without any noticeable impact on Guinea or Ghana"), when there were allegations of attacks on Uganda from the Sudan as well as from Tanzania, and when all sorts of dire rumors were being aired about British, American, and Israeli designs on Uganda's sovereign integrity. (The United States and Israel were both incriminated through the same vehicles—six Second-World-War Sherman tanks under Amin's command. Nobody bothered to explain how they had got there: America had conveyed them under Lend-lease to the Soviet Union, which when they became obsolete for Russian purposes had passed them along to Egypt, which had let them be captured during the Six-Day War by Israel, which in turn had no use for them and had given them to Uganda.)

Despite the air of tension that still prevailed, or that foreigners expected to prevail, in Kampala, General Amin's place was wide open. I drove up by taxi, was waved by a guard into the courtyard, and, without anybody's asking me to identify myself, walked into his house and upstairs. I came upon a colorful scene. The victorious soldier was receiving the nation's commanding churchmen, and they were assembled on his second-story verandah—Muslims and Christians in all their finery, even a rabbi, and a starchy couple, he black, she white, in Salvation Army regalia. Obote had customarily kept people who had appointments with him waiting for forty-five minutes. Amin, apparently determined to outdo his predecessor, now kept the religious elders waiting, under a fierce midday sun, for exactly one hour. A Muslim himself, with four wives, he looked cool when he arrived. He was wearing a short-sleeved open-collar shirt that exposed his enormous neck and arms. For eight years, he had been heavyweight champion of the Ugandan army, in which he had enlisted when he was sixteen. Towering over his guests, he looked as though he could still lick anybody in the house. He had a soft smile, as if he had just eaten something—a country, perhaps—that had agreed with him. Once, in reading a prepared statement, which he did simply and awkwardly, he burped.

He had little of substance to say. He expressed his belief in "the equality and brotherhood of man and peace and good will on earth" (polite applause) and pledged that the "new republic will allow total religious freedom to anybody without any fear or favor" (louder applause), and he closed by saying he'd acted as he had "for God and my country." He had used the line the day before while freeing fifty-five of Obote's political prisoners. This humanitarian gesture was in the classic tradition of military coups, and a few days later Amin would show further evidence that he was being fast shaped in the conventional strong-man mold: He all at once promised free elections, sometime soon, banned all political activity for two years, and dissolved Parliament. When, a week or so after that, he got around to appointing a new cabinet, it was made up entirely of civilians, but he announced they would all be expected to take military training.

After the session with the churchmen, I went back downtown to look up the friend who'd previously taken me to the Uganda Club. I had been wondering what, considering his intimate connections with the old guard, might have happened to him. He was not at his office. An associate told me he'd gone out to coffee, and added that he had been seen marching jubilantly in a pro-Amin demonstration, which surprised me. My man was a long time in returning from his coffee break. "I've lost my friends in the cabinet," he explained when he finally showed up, "so I've been out making new ones." Back at the Apolo Hotel, I bumped into the two beer salesmen, both of them wearing ear-to-ear smiles; the curfew hadn't hurt sales a bit, one of them told me, because people were simply filling their habitual quotas in the middle of the day —and in not a few instances, indeed, attaining new, euphoric levels of consumption. I boarded an elevator along with a conspicuously sober, turbaned Asian, and as we soared up in our Apolo capsule I asked him how he felt about all the developments of the past few days. "What's done's done," he said. "Now everything depends on God." And, as General Amin would surely have been the first to agree, on country.

13

The change of government in Uganda had a rippling effect throughout East Africa. In conservative Ethiopia, which had found itself ringed by mountingly anti-imperialist and bellicose neighbors (and which had its own left-wing insurrection waged by the Eritrean Liberation Front), Amin's move to counter the Move to the Left was welcomed. In radical Sudan, which has common boundaries with Ethiopia and Uganda, and which had been engaging in border skirmishes with both, the coup was deplored. But its chief external impact was to jeopardize the future of one of the few on-going regional associations of a continent whose prospects seem to many to be crucially dependent on an international, rather than national, approach to the solution of political and economic problems—to the future, that was, of the East African Community. This organization, which had been in existence since December, 1967, was itself the successor to a body established by the British in 1948 to provide joint services for their principal dependencies in the area.

The Community, set up by Uganda, Kenya, and Tanzania, had as its supreme authority the presidents of its three member states. After the coup, President Nyerere, who was not only playing host to Obote but still recognized him as the legitimate head of the Ugandan government, could hardly be expected to sit down comfortably with General Amin and discuss common matters. So the Community limped along, functioning as best it could under its permanent civil servants, until Kenya's Kenyatta worked out a face-saving compromise: documents that had to be endorsed by the three presidents would be signed first by himself and Nyerere, who would thus never be officially aware that Amin was signing them too. A further complication was that from its start the Community's headquarters had been in the northern Tanzanian city of Arusha, a spot chosen because it lay almost precisely in the geographical center of the troika nations and also almost precisely halfway between Cairo and Cape Town, Africa's polar metropolises.

Arusha was not otherwise an ideal setting. It is off the beaten East African track. Ambitious public servants from all three member countries are loath to be posted there, since it means that they can't easily participate in the power struggles back in their own capitals; more than one aspiring individual who has fallen into temporary disfavor at home has found himself quickly sent to Arusha, whence the sound of a nagging voice doesn't carry far. Still, big things were expected of the Community, and at the very moment of the Uganda uprising negotiations were under way for the expansion of its facilities in the form of a seventeen-million-dollar building program at Arusha. Eight thousand Community employees work there now, and another sixty thousand or so are deployed throughout the three countries attending to the Community's principal responsibilities—railways and harbors, the East African Airways, and posts and communications. (The Community countries have exemplary telephone service; during the flare-up in Uganda, there was no difficulty getting through to Kampala from Nairobi or Dar es Salaam.)

Beyond all that, the Community serves as the collector, for all three nations, of income taxes and excise duties. Under it, too, is a tri-national Court of Appeals, albeit with limited jurisdiction; it does not pass on constitutional questions. The Community runs an aviation school and has under its aegis several regional research centers—in fisheries, in agriculture, in veterinary medicine, in meteorology. A footnote to East African Community history was a visit in 1970 by its Secretary General, a Ugandan, to still another of its research installations, an Institute of Malaria and Vector-borne Diseases; while he was inspecting the premises, the staff inspected him and discovered that *he* had malaria.

Before the coup in Uganda, the Community's proponents had high hopes for it. To begin with, overtures had been made to several prospective new members: Burundi, Somalia, and, more consequentially, Ethiopia and Zambia. And whether or not any of them joined up, there was to have been an intensification of economic cooperation among the three founding nations. A complicated system of "transfer taxes" had been instituted, the net effect of which was to be to give Uganda and Tanzania, traditionally the poorer relations in this triumviral family, a chance to catch up with rich brother Kenya. There were detailed studies under way to establish, within the Community, strategic industries—automotive, chemical, iron-and-steel—that could not operate profitably without a common market in all three countries.

But, as had proved to be the case in West Africa also, nationalism outweighed rationalism. Uganda manufactured enough textiles to supply the whole area; but then Tanzania, with considerable help from Peking, started up a Chinese Friendship Mill, and Kenya promptly moved into that field itself. Indeed, by early 1971, the Community had made little economic progress, and there were some who thought that the three countries were less communal than they had been under colonialism. The British had had a single currency for the region. Now, there were separate currencies, with all sorts of barriers against their interchangeability. The underlying trouble, political differences aside, was that while the Community members were about equal in population (Tanzania: twelve million, Uganda: eleven million, Kenya: ten million), Kenya had long overshadowed its partners, financially and industrially. The government leaders in Kampala and Dar es Salaam were suffering, as had other Ugandans and Tanzanians before them, from what is known in East Africa as the Nairobi syndrome.

Under the British, Nairobi had unarguably been the transportation and communications hub of East Africa, and it still was. Foreign industrialists have long been leery of making substantial investments in Africa, which strikes them as a confusing, unpredictable area. The Bata Shoe Company has done very well in East Africa, but a perhaps apochryphal story about the genesis of its involvement illustrates the bewilderment so often experienced by outsiders. According to the legend, the company sent two emissaries to Africa to size it up as a possible sales market. One reported back that it was hopeless, since nobody there wore shoes; the other that it had limitless potentialities, since nobody there wore shoes. Those foreign companies that, like Bata, have decided to set up factories or sales offices in East Africa have almost always done so in or near Nairobi, which has excellent plane service, an agreeably high altitude and moderate climate, and an aura of cosmopolitanism far beyond anything Kampala or Dar es Salaam can offer. Uganda and Tanzania had hopes when they entered into the Community that the partnership would reduce the historical trade gap between them and Kenya, but instead it broadened. In 1969, for instance, Kenya sold thirty-one million dollars' worth of goods to Tanzania and bought only four million dollars' worth.

The motto of Kenya today is "Harambee," Swahili for "Pull together" or "Heave ho." President Kenyatta has his Nairobi offices in Harambee House, on Harambee Avenue. But within the East African Community, the harambee spirit has been little evident. While Uganda and Tanzania have jealously watched Kenya get the lion's share of the regional spoils, Kenya, for its part, has been wondering what the other two are up to in their relations with countries further afield. In Nairobi, there is a small diplomatic mission from Peking so carefully watched that its members rarely stray far from their quarters, and two Kenyans received eighteen-month prison terms merely for having Mao books in their possession; Tanzania abounds not only with Chinese writings but with Chinese, who are building a railroad from there to Zambia. How does that sort of activity jibe, Kenyans ask dourly, with the existing East African rail network run by the Community? Why, the new line won't even have a compatible track gauge!

Nevertheless, despite all its woes, the East African Community has managed, albeit shakily, to survive. To break it up would require the duplication, or triplication, of its existing common services, and that would be prohibitively expensive. So the three member states have stuck together—much in the manner, some think, of the partners in an unhappy marriage who can't afford a divorce—out of the pragmatic realization that their mutual interests are even stronger than their individual inclinations.

It is sometimes said of His Imperial Majesty Haile Selassie I that in his half-century's reign he has managed to lead that bedraggled, feudal country all the way from the twelfth century into the thirteenth. When Jomo Kenyatta took over the reins in Kenya, his problem was similar to that of most of the other black African heads of state—to guide their people in one big leap from the nineteenth century into the twenty-first. Kenyatta became president of independent Kenya in 1963. He had previously spent nine years in a British prison. When he took over, because of the Mau Mau incidents with which he and his followers were so closely identified, the British thought blood would run in Kenyan streets. Now Kenyata has such a firm grip on his country that the British and others are horrified when he catches a cold. Some people claim that he doesn't rule; he reigns.

Kenyatta, who turned eighty-one in 1971 and is called "Mzee"— Swahili for "Elder"—is so supreme that, unlike many of his contemporary leaders, he does not have to engage in revolutionary rhetoric to maintain his position; he is one of the few around who can make a political speech on so tame a theme as the virtues of hard work. His age notwithstanding, he has been bouncing all over the country, with his ever-present fly whisk. Naturally, he is mortal, and there are those Kenyans who gloomily expect that his death will lead to civil war. Others are less pessimistic. "When Kenyatta goes," one government man in Nairobi told me, "we're not going to run around slitting each other's throats, no matter how much that might please some outsiders. We know what we want, and that's continued stability. We're not going to mess up our country."

Along with being the *mzee* of the country, Kenyatta is the *mzee* as well of its dominant tribe, the Kikuyus. There are numerous small tribes in Kenya—the vice-president, Daniel arap Moi, is a Kalenjin, as is the local folk hero, Kipchoge Keino, the brightest star in the country's galaxy of distance runners—but the country is mainly run by its two million Kikuyus. They occupy six of its cabinet ministries and nine of its twenty-two permanent secretary-ships. The Kikuyus are like the Ibos of Nigeria or the Ashanti of Ghana; they are the people who get things done. Energetic, tough, and arrogant, they led the fight for independence. They have a distinct tribal psyche, and have been described as a cross between Jews and Scotsmen.

There are marked differences between them and their principal rivals, the Luos, who number one million, three hundred thousand. Kikuyus circumcize; Luos don't. Kikuyus inherit patrilineally, Luos matrilineally. The Luos are determinedly tribal. They won't let their sons marry women in whose families there has been a suicide or deliberate murder—casual homicide doesn't count—or where there has been a history of persistent inadequate cultivation of subsistence food. "First and foremost, an African must know who he is," a sophisticated Luo woman in Nairobi told me. "I could stay in Europe or America all my life, but I'd still remain a Luo." Luos teach their children their own language before either English or Swahili. Tom Mboya, a contender to inherit Ken-yatta's mantle until he was assassinated, in still murky circum-stances, in the fall of 1969, was a Luo. Still another is Oginga Odinga, who was for a while Kenya's vice-president, but who after Mboya's death, at a time when disgruntled Luos were throwing stones at Kenyatta, was put in prison, and was not released for eighteen months. The Luos are considered the intelligentsia of Kenya, but Oginga Odinga was an exception. He never had much formal schooling, and because of that he employed a young, not especially political, compatriot to go over his speeches and cor-respondence and fix up his grammar and spelling. The security police arrested him too.

Kenyatta has brought Kenya economic as well as political stability, and has done so in large part by retaining, even courting, the services of expatriates. By 1982, according to the country's latest national development plan, it is hoped that all noncitizens will be phased out of jobs in the high and middle manpower echelons; but by 1972 the country still expects that of one hundred and ninety-one architects it will need only forty will be Kenyans; and that as of the same date there will be a short-fall of two hundred and forty-one people in the "artists, writers, and related" category.

Kenya goes in for meticulous planning. Much of its attention has been focused lately on the redistribution of land. In the colonial days, most of the good acreage belonged to Europeans. In the last five years, two hundred and fifty thousand Africans have been resettled on expropriated land. (Some of the English settlers are still around. Once within the boundaries of the Duke of Manchester's estate, two hundred and sixty miles north of Nairobi, the visitor has yet an eighteen-mile drive to reach the ducal residence.) "When we were growing up and being educated by missionaries who said our tribal dances were reprehensible, and taught us to read Shakespeare, we not only didn't have any land, we didn't have any cultural identity," one Kenyan official told me. "Now we are getting back our land and we can stop imitating the whites and we can say, with real meaning, 'I'm a Kenyan!'" (How they say it—"Kennyan" or "Keenyan"—depends on where they went to school and whom they are addressing; talking to another Kenyan, the same man may say "Kennyan" who, talking to a foreign diplomat, will switch to "Keenyan.")

The purpose of the land-settlement program is to give Kenyan farmers a chance to find and glory in their own freeholding identity, but much of the choice land, especially near Nairobi, has notwithstanding come into the hands of government officials who seem to acquire estates and Mercedes limousines with relative ease. Not only do they have steady incomes but they can get government loans. Several months ago, moreover, the members of the Kenyan parliament concurrently imposed a freeze on ordinary people's wages and voted themselves what amounted to a hundred-percent increase in pay. At the end of 1970, when there was a parliamentary election, a taxi driver in Nairobi told a friend of mine that he wasn't going to participate, and when he was asked the reason, he said, "Why should I? I've been voting for ten years and all the people I've put into office are buying farms and houses now, and I'm still driving a cab."

The Kenyan Ambassador to the United States was at a party in Washington not long ago and, on being introduced to a new acquaintance, was told, "Glad to meet you. I know you're over here representing the finest animals in the world." "Yes, and we have eleven million people, too," the Ambassador replied. It is a fact, though, that the people's welfare depends in part on the animals. Tourism, which brought fifty million dollars in revenue to Kenya last year, is of enormous importance to the entire East African economy. Curiously, it wasn't even mentioned in the 125-page treaty that Kenya, Uganda, and Tanzania signed in 1967 when they formed the East African Community. Now the three of them are spiritedly competing for tourist revenue. So is nearby Ethiopia. Trying to drain off some of the money that Kenya earns from this source, Ethiopia has been handing out free visas at airports, and in eight years its annual influx of tourists has risen from six hundred to fifty thousand.

Ugandans are forever asking foreigners, "Don't you think our game parks are nicer than *theirs?*" As for Tanzania, it has set aside nearly one quarter of its three hundred and sixty-five thousand square miles for animal reserves. In Tanzania, where President Nyerere has declared that the survival of wild life is a matter of grave concern not only to Africa "but the rest of the world as well," the Society for the Prevention of Cruelty to Animals solicits small-coin contributions with rhinoceros banks instead of piggy banks. It is a constant source of irritation there that its principal wild-animal areas—the Serengeti Plain, the Ngorongoro Crater, and Lake Manyara—produce more income for Kenya than for Tanzania, inasmuch as most safaris are booked out of Nairobi and paid for in advance. In 1970, a hundred and forty thousand tourists, thirty-eight thousand of them from the United States, were credited to Kenya, and only forty thousand to Tanzania. True, there is some ambivalence in the latter country about the circumstance that in a black socialist nation the overwhelming majority of visitors to its game parks are rich whites. One sees posters in Dar es Salaam showing a black man taking his children to look at giraffes and zebras, and the Tanzanian government provides special buses and hostels in the reserve areas for indigenes; but very few of them avail themselves of the opportunity, and one Tanzanian professor told me that no African would dream of visiting a game park except to indulge the whim of a foreign guest.

What upsets Tanzanians most of all is the unscrupulosity—or ignorance—of travel agents around the world, and even of a few mapmakers, who jointly pretend that Mount Kilimanjaro is in Kenya and not, as it actually is, in Tanzania. The famous mountain, capped the year round by Africa's only snow, means so much to Tanzanians that on the day they became independent they made sure their new flag was hoisted at its summit; the Chief of Staff of the Tanzanian Army has made an annual pilgrimage to the top for a dozen years. And here is Kenya claiming it! Now, even though Tanzania probably can't afford it, the country has built an international airport near Kilimanjaro; the idea was to persuade airlines to fly tourists directly there from Europe rather than, as had regularly been the practice, to Nairobi.

Many of these visitors will undoubtedly come from West Germany. Even today, it is sometimes hard to get a clear look at a lion in an East African game park because of all the Germans surrounding it. After the Uganda coup, when the border to Kenya was opened up to traffic, the first vehicle across was a busload of German tourists. Willy Brandt spent a 1971 holiday in East Africa and predicted, soberingly, that many more of his countrymen would follow his example. A single Tanzanian travel agency already has ninety-eight Germans booked every week through 1978. There is historical justification for the Germans' interest in that country. They used to own Tanganyika, its mainland component. The Kaiser had a winter home there. Even today, a Lutheran Theological College stands near the Arusha National Park, and Dar es Salaam has a big Lutheran church that would look at home in Nuremberg.

But the Kenyan ambassador to Washington was understandably dismayed by the implication that his countrymen consider wild animals their highest-priority asset. The fact is that the animal most Africans care most about is the cow. Kenyans, for instance, have a special branch of the national police called the Stock Theft Unit, and the Nairobi newspapers are full of stories about dastardly Ethiopian cattle rustlers who have swooped across the border. At the University of Nairobi, a new research institute called the International Center of Insect Physiology and Ecology is getting under way, and much of its attention is being focused on two cattle predators, the tick and the tsetse fly. Under the direction of a black Ph.D. in cell biology and insect physiology from Cambridge University, Dr. Thomas Odhiambo, the Center has the ultimate goal of eradicating, or at least curbing, these two pesky enemies of Africa, not to mention the termite, the army worm, and the mosquito. If only the tick and tsetse fly could be vanquished, Dr. Odhiambo believes, Africa could almost overnight become a cattle-exporting area of the dimensions of Uruguay or Argentina.

Among the chief beneficiaries of the success of the Center could be still another large East African tribe, the legendary Masai of Kenya and northern Tanzania, whose diet consists almost exclusively of the meat and milk and blood of their cattle. Although many of them live near game preserves, they do not eat wild animals, and they only hunt lions or leopards that attack their herds. Tall, thin, and striking-looking, the Masai, in their red and orange robes, have by now had so many encounters with tourists that they have attained a high measure of sophistication. When, for example, I gave a lift to one spear-carrying warrior, he graciously agreed to be photographed, after a seven-mile free ride, for merely a shilling—a drastic reduction of the usual fee. Just before he set out to walk across a trackless plain, toward an invisible destination, I asked how he had got an ugly scar that ran from eye to ear. From a leopard, he said. His spear, which had seemed very long and menacing, suddenly looked quite frail.

The Masai have limited access to water. One social anthropologist whose first visit to them, in 1961, happened to coincide with a providential downpour, has been revered by them ever since as a rainmaker. They generally use what water they have for drinking, instead of washing, and as a result they attract as many flies as their cattle do; they have learned to endure this torment, and they often do not bother to brush off insects even when they are perched on their eyes. The Masai homes are dark round huts made of mud and cow dung, and to the uninitiated these people look like primitivism personified, but along with so many other Africans they are rapidly changing their traditional ways. The first indigenous atomic physicist from Kenya—if he maintains his present rate of study—will be a Masai. And when a poll was taken not long ago among some of them, to find out what aspirations they had for the future, eighty percent of those who responded said they hoped their children would become members of Parliament.

14

In its relations with the white world, Kenya is unique among black African countries. Before independence, there was nowhere on the continent—save South Africa and Rhodesia—a comparable white presence. Because of its exposure to the white settlers, Kenya enjoyed an edge over the rest of independent black Africa in agriculture and industry. It can provide almost all the amenities of European life—in housing, in food, in transportation, in schools, in recreation—and this has been one of the reasons why foreign investors are so attracted to it, along with the representatives of international agencies (WHO, ILO, FAO, and so on) who must find some place for their families to live and who not unreasonably pick the one that is most homelike.

Today there are only forty thousand European residents in Kenya, and while they still play a consequential role in its affairs, they are no longer all-important. I made a pilgrimage one day to Isak Dinesen's home, half an hour's drive from Nairobi, the scene of *Out of Africa*. The town she lived in now bears her Christian name, Karen, but when I asked at the local police station for directions to her house, none of the men there had heard of her pen name or of Baroness Blixen, nor did they have any idea how

Karen had got its name. The author left Africa in 1932, and since 1966, through a gift from the people of Denmark, her home, with the Ngong Hills she loved still visible from its terrace, has been used as a domestic-science school for African girls, with a Danish woman as headmistress. Nearby is a memorial to Denys Finch-hatton, Miss Dinesen's friend who was killed in a plane crash; a copper plaque identifying him has long since been removed, supposedly by Masai who used the metal to make ornaments for their impressively distended ear lobes.

Almost all the expatriates remaining in Kenya are British. More than two thousand of them are employed by the Kenyan civil service. Most of the judges in Kenya's courts, including the Chief Justice, are British, and the Africans are by and large rather pleased with this arrangement; they think that with expatriates on the bench they get a fairer shake. (Nowhere in Africa does one find much pronounced *dislike* of the former colonial masters. The foreigners most popular in Ethiopia today are Italians; in Addis Ababa, as I was strolling past the Banco di Roma Ethiopia one day with an Ethiopian acquaintance, he looked at it and remarked, "I sometimes wish we hadn't fought them too hard to give them more of a chance to help us.") And there are numerous nongovernmental expatriate organizations in Kenya, like the Flying Doctors Society of Africa. Privately supported and based in Nairobi, it furnishes regular and emergency medical services to a six-hundred-thousand-square-mile stretch of Kenya, Uganda, and Tanzania—an area about the size of western Europe, an area, moreover, in which the per-capita government outlay for health amounts to a dollar a year, and in which there is one nonflying doctor for every thirty thousand people. When it comes to that, there are more doctors in White Plains, New York, than in all of Ethiopia—a country in which, incidentally, a flabbergasted European doctor within a single week had his first exposure to non-laboratory cases of yellow fever, cholera, smallpox, and plague.

The Flying Doctors Society has built a network of one hundred landing strips in its territory, and it serves sixty-five rural hospitals, each of which calls in by radio at a specific hour every day. The core of its staff consists of twenty doctors, five of them full-time and three of these pilots. Assisted by five additional pilots, they log altogether three hundred and fifty thousand miles and a couple of thousand operations annually. They charge no fees; if a patient has any money, he is invited to make a donation to the Society. Its founder was a British doctor, A. Michael Wood, himself a pilot. Now a citizen of Tanzania, he has a wheat-and-cattle farm on the lower slopes of Mount Kilimanjaro. Dr. Wood's specialty is plastic surgery, and he has found ample opportunities to practice it, inasmuch as many of the emergencies with which he and his colleagues cope involve uneven encounters between man and beast—this patient bitten by a crocodile, that one by a hippo. The Flying Doctors patched up one woman who had been carried three miles on an elephant tusk, and another who had walked sixty miles for help after being gored in the stomach by a rhino; not long ago, they treated a couple of American tourists who had somehow got themselves impaled on buffalo horns. "It is encouraging to see aircraft being used for constructive human tasks," Dr. Wood said laconically in the Society's annual report, "instead of dropping bombs and napalm."

One of the larger groups of expatriates still resident in East Africa is Asians. Most of their forebears came to the continent, at the turn of the twentieth century, from India, where they were recruited to construct railroads for the British; most of the descendants became shopkeepers. At independence time in Kenya, of forty thousand small stores in the country, about one quarter were owned by Asians. In Nairobi, there is one whole street lined from end to end with Indian warehouses, and the room in the Nairobi Museum where Dr. Louis S. B. Leakey's celebrated *Kenyapithicus Africanus* discovery is on view is called Mahatma Gandhi Hall.

When independence came to Kenya, on December 12, 1963, the Asians, like all other foreigners who had lived there for at least five years, were given two years to become, if they chose, fullfledged citizens of the new country. (Among the expatriates who exercised this option was Dr. Leakey.) Of the Asians who did apply for citizenship, several came to hold prominent positions in the government. Quick among those to avail themselves of the opportunity were the followers of the Aga Khan, who has one hundred thousand disciples in East Africa, twenty-five thousand of them in Kenya. (The bird room in the Nairobi museum is named after him.) They were enjoined by their spiritual ruler to take out citizenship, to become "part and parcel" of the nation, in the words of their Kenyan leader, Sir Eboo Pirbhai, who runs a travel agency in Nairobi and has been, since 1952, the only knighted Asian in Kenya.

Sir Eboo is not the only successful member of his sect. In 1945, the then Aga Khan advised his subjects that petty shop-keeping was outmoded, and that they should set their sights higher and get involved in every phase of community life. Many of them did. They went into all sorts of businesses—the Aga Khan himself owns Nairobi's leading newspaper—and they established their own hospital and their own school system. They felt involved in Kenya, and they felt secure there, and they were happy to become Kenyans.

It was not so with most other Asians in the area. At independence time, many of them were apprehensive. They remembered the Mau Mau assaults on foreigners. More immediately, they were appalled by events on the island of Zanzibar, to their southeast. Zanzibar—before it was merged into Tanzania—became independent on December 11, 1963, just one day ahead of Kenya. A month later, there was an outbreak of xenophobic violence in the island republic, and twelve thousand people were slaughtered, nearly all of them Asians. Then the Congo became independent, and the butchery there sent streams of Belgian refugees into East Africa, scared and penniless.

All this gave the Asians in Kenya pause. They weren't worried about their safety as long as Kenyatta was around, but what if something happened to him? So they decided to watch and wait; after all, they had two years to make up their minds, and many of them had British passports, so they figured they could always go to England. The upshot was that only about twenty thousand ever filed for citizenship—three quarters of these just under the wire. Five years afterward, five thousand of the last-minute applications were still unprocessed, even though some Asians who applied after the two-year period of grace had managed meanwhile to obtain citizenship, usually by bribery. Subsequently the government, through its control of trade licenses and work permits (there are now some seventy commodities in which noncitizens may not traffic, ranging from shoelaces and razor blades to Ovaltine and rat traps), began to make things difficult for the Asians who had chosen to remain aliens, and it did so in rather helter-skelter fashion. In 1966, it ordered three thousand Asians to close their shops, among these a number of individuals who *had* become citizens. On one Nairobi street there were five stores, four of them owned by Indian noncitizens and the other by an Indian citizen; the only one who was forced out of business was the citizen. In the last couple of years, the government has been less energetic about harassing the Asian shopkeepers, in part because Africans have not shown the anticipated eagerness to assume their roles in trade.

Added to all this was the disposition of many Africans to dislike Asians, citizenship notwithstanding. The Asians, aside from the Aga Khan contingent, had for the most part kept to themselves; they were rumored to be rich; they inspired the same suspicion and distrust that blacks in Harlem have felt toward Jewish shopkeepers there. So at the end of 1965, some of the East African Asians began to pack up and move to England. The number that migrated was actually not very large—probably six thousand in 1966, another six thousand in 1967, and twelve thousand in 1968. But their exodus was widely publicized, so there seemed to be multitudes of immigrants. If one Asian left Nairobi, fifty relatives and friends would see him off, and the television coverage of his departure would show an airport swarming with Asians. Another fifty would meet him in London: same pictures, same inferences. Then Enoch Powell got the British panicky by talking about a wave of immigration, and the Asians' fear that Britain would shut its doors to them in turn produced a *real* wave of sorts; in the first two months of 1969, nearly twenty thousand of them headed for England.

Meanwhile, Great Britain began passing restrictive immigration laws against their entry, British passports or no British passports, and to the Asians still in Africa these laws were manifestly unfair. The top priority for permission to stay permanently in England was accorded to those Asians already in prison there on a charge of illegal entry. The next priority went to paupers. If an Indian shopkeeper in Kenya had a few thousand pounds saved up, he couldn't pass the destitution test; after waiting two years, spending his savings, unable to earn more money, finally wiped out, and humiliated by living off the charity of his friends, he could *then* go to England—but no longer with any capital to help him get started there.

The hundred and fifty thousand Asians who remain in East Africa feel put upon, and their prospects are bleak. Two thousand of them worked as clerks and tellers in Nairobi banks, where their presence had always grated on Africans, who were in constant need of money, believed that the banks controlled most of the money around, and could see for themselves that the people *handling* the money were Asians. By 1972, the government of Kenya expects that the bank staffs will be totally Africanized, and the Asians who worked there will be hard pressed to find other jobs. Immigration to England is still a possibility. That country has changed its laws several times, but in mid-1971 was admitting ten thousand Asians annually from the entire Commonwealth.

Those who elect to remain in East Africa will probably not starve to death. Like Africans, they have an extended-family system, and enough of them are still earning money enough to provide, skimpily, for all of them. But their pride has suffered. The Kenyan government, for its part, feels that it is too bad that the Asians are in such a fix, but that their dilemma is largely of their own making; after all, they did have the two years to obtain citizenship. When I asked one government official in Nairobi what, if anything, the administration planned to do about the plight of the Asians, he shrugged and said, "It is the responsibility of any sovereign state to give priority, as I believe yours does, too, to its own citizens."

Tanzania also has an Asian problem. There are some seventy-five thousand Asians still living there. In Dar es Salaam, where the incumbent Aga Khan was ceremoniously installed as Imam of the Age in 1957, hundreds of Indians gather at the waterfront at dusk, gossiping, philosophizing, and gazing at the lights of the ships at anchor in the harbor. The Asians' lot in Tanzania has been easier, on the whole, than that of those in Kenya. Tanzania never had a dominant expatriate-settler class, and as a result there had been no tendency for its Asians, unlike Kenya's, to function as buffers between lordly whites and lowly blacks. For all Tanzania's praiseworthy espousal of egalitarian principles, however, its Asians are still regarded a a class apart: As in colonial days, three kinds of food are served today in Tanzanian prisons—African, European, and Asian. (Many prisoners in Tanzania work on farms and in factories. By some, this practice is viewed as evidence of an enlightened policy; by others, as a questionable reliance on cheap, forced labor.)

In the fall of 1970, the Tanzanian government instituted some new regulations on overseas travel that made it difficult for its citizens to be educated abroad. Ostensibly, the purpose was to conserve foreign exchange; actually, it was interpreted by many wealthy Asians as a slap against them, since they were the ones who had most frequently indicated that they thought their children could get a better education abroad than at home. In the spring of 1971, moreover, Tanzania nationalized all buildings worth more than one hundred thousand shillings (fourteen thousand dollars), and much of the property that was affected by the sudden action belonged, as it happened, to Asians. Among the twenty-nine hundred structures involved was a two-million-dollar one belonging to the Aga Khan, at the unveiling of which just a few months earlier President Nyerere had put in a ceremonial appearance.

Earlier, the country's importing and exporting businesses, in which Asians figured prominently, had been largely supplanted by state trading agencies. One of these, the National Milling Corporation, is managed by an African-born Asian, J. K. Chande, who is quite content with his new lot. Under free enterprise, he ran one company; under socialism, he runs nine. He has charge of the country's entire production of wheat flour and animal feed, and of sixty percent of the production of rice and corn flour. His parastatal organization also controls canned mangos, pineapples, tomato juice, orange juice, jams, and spices, not to mention a wine factory that was started years ago by missionaries.

Chande took the job with the cheerful expectation of being Africanized out of it in two years, in keeping with the national pattern: Eighty percent of Tanzania's retail stores, most of which once had Asian proprietors, are now supposedly run by blacks. The announced percentage seems high, for there remains a very visible Asian shopkeeping presence. I drove north from Dar one day, for instance, to the coastal town of Bagamoyo, the old slave port from which Henry Stanley set forth to find Dr. Livingstone, and to which, on February 24, 1874, Livingstone's body was delivered by African porters after a fifteen-hundred-mile march from the interior that took them nine months. I arrived at lunch time, and the only source of any kind of food proved to be a small Indian-run store with some biscuits and cheese and tinned beef and beer blessedly in stock.

15

Like Kenya, Tanzania, on becoming independent, offered all its residents, whatever their ethnic origins, a chance to become citizens. Again, not all availed themselves of the opportunity. There are about twenty thousand Europeans still around, of whom only two-hundred-odd are citizens. One who is not, an Englishman with a good government job, told me he expected to stay in Tanzania as long as a white man could find employment, but that becoming a Tanzanian was something else again. "What if war should break out?" he said. Much more optimistic, and more chauvinistic, was the behavior of Lady Marion Chesham, the daughter of a Philadelphia lawyer, who is a member of the Tanzanian parliament. On the day when applications for citizenship were first accepted, she arose early so she could stand at the head of the line, only to be thwarted by an even more patriotic Asian who sneaked into the registration office by a back door. Lady Chesham is the widow of a British peer who for close to a quarter of a century, while living in Britain, was, in the House of Lords, a staunch and lonely advocate of Tanganyikan independence. "He wasn't very popular because of that, poor devil," Lady Chesham says. "He was a bit ahead of his time, but by God, everything he said would happen eventually did happen." The Cheshams moved to Tanganyika in 1946, and operated a farm at Aringa, in the southwest highlands of the territory. Tanganyika's own chief advocate of independence, Julius Nyerere, made a speech there one day in the early 1950s, and Lady Chesham sought him out afterward, got to know him, and in support of his aspirations ran for the colonial parliament in 1958. She has been a prominent MP ever since—today, one of the four Europeans, and one of the nine women, in the federal legislature.

From the start, in Africa, Lady Chesham was interested in community development. After her husband's death, in 1952, she gave their farm to their employees, and the main house became a training center for woman village leaders. Lately she has been a vigorous and articulate proponent of Nyerere's socialistic program, which is called "Ujamaa," a Swahili word that means "Family-hood" or "We live together." Lady Chesham has defined it in her own words. "Ujamaa is a way of thinking, a concept by which those who have advantages in life do not use these advantages to exploit the poor but rather to help them," she declared not long ago. "Ujamaa is *noblesse oblige* brought into everyday life. The greater the privileges, the greater the responsibilities. Ujamaa brings hope and progress to the unprivileged so that all the people work together. Ujamaa builds one People, one Nation. Ujamaa is a way of life. It has been preached to the world for two thousand years. We in Tanzania are trying to live it. Webster's Dictionary defines the word 'community' as 'a community of interests causing people to work together.' Another definition is 'sharing together a community of ideas.' This also is *ujamaa*."

Tanzania's *ujamaa* program got under way in 1969. Its people had never been much interested in communal living. Only four of its one hundred and twenty tribes went in for nucleated settlements; most of the indigenes were spread out across the land, farming four- or five-acre plots for their own sustenance. Nyerere believed that if the country was going to make much headway he would have to reverse an urban population flow that was gradually increasing and, moreover, would have to merge the rural people into larger social units. Even before independence he had tried to do something about the latter through his political party, the Tanganyika African National Union. Starting in 1958, he began organizing what were known as TANU Youth League Settlements.

The idea was that the government would give young folk some cleared land, and would furnish advisers they might need to help them in areas like agriculture and animal husbandry. Hundreds of such settlements were organized, but the British were cool to the scheme, and the participants, with no money, no skills, and as yet not much feeling of national pride, got discouraged and went back to their former homes. By 1966, two years after independence, there were only half a dozen of these settlements left. Undismayed, Nyerere shortly proclaimed a *ujamaa* village program, which was similar to the old one but more socialistically oriented. By the summer of 1969, it was operative. By mid-1970, there were eleven hundred *ujamaa* villages; by mid-1971, more than two thousand. The smallest village had seven inhabitants; the largest, twenty-eight hundred. The *ujamaa* villages have been compared with the kibbutzim of Israel, but there are notable differences. In a kibbutz, communal feeding and communal child care are the customary practice. In Africa, the family is a unit the integrity of which no government would lightly challenge.

Nyerere's *ujamaa* village program is also supervised by his political party. The government gives TANU seventeen million shillings a year (about two and a half million dollars) to spend on the villages, in all of which more than eight hundred thousand Tanzanians now live, the majority of them in homes made of mud, sticks, and thatch. En route from Dar es Salaam to Bagamoyo, I dropped in at one called Kerege. It had a population of seven hundred and ninety-one, divided into a hundred and sixty-three families. They jointly owned seven thousand acres; so far, they had only two thousand acres under cultivation, which was ample for their needs. For communal consumption, they were growing cocoa, rice, maize, cassava, bananas, and beans. In addition, each family had a one-acre plot of its own on which it could raise whatever it wished. The village, by Western lights, looked austere, but its residents were proud of being able to share three tractors, a herd of dairy cattle that produced twenty-five gallons of milk a day, a football field, an elementary school, an Anglican church, and a mosque. There was a community center in the planning stage. The village was run by a democratically elected executive committee with five subcommittees under it—for livestock, agriculture, construction, finances, and social-and-cultural affairs—and under them a number of working groups, to one of which each adult member of the community was assigned, and by which his daily duties were prescribed.

Every *ujamaa* community is supposed to develop a cash crop; Kerege's was cashew nuts. The villagers had built themselves a cement-block processing plant, and were handling two hundred tons of nuts a year—fifty tons from four hundred and fifty of their own acres that they had reserved for cashew trees, the rest from nearby communes that didn't have plants of their own. They marketed their nuts (which would ultimately sell in New York at two and a half dollars a pound, retail) through the National Agricultural Products Board. At the end of each year, whatever money the village had earned—the bulk of it a twenty-four-percent share of the wholesale cashew-nut proceeds—is distributed, after certain deductions for the common weal, according to the number of days an individual has worked. Last year, the minimum per capita income was one hundred and twenty dollars and the maximum one hundred and forty—a modest sum, but slightly above the national average for Tanzanian farmers. The villagers I spoke to seemed quite content, and one of the things that appeared to have contributed to their morale was that they had twice been honored by personal visits from the man chiefly responsible for their being there—President Nyerere.

Nyerere is known throughout Africa as a statesman of pronounced intellectual bent. As Kenyatta is called "Mzee," he is "Mwalimo," which means "teacher" in Swahili. The title is in such widespread use that it even precedes Nyerere's name in the official government directory. On a continent many of whose leaders are celebrated for their lavish style of living and love of pageantry, he is an anomaly. He has confounded onlookers by insisting that his chauffeur stop for red lights. On a continent where the still not fully slaked thirst for self-government has produced time-consuming costly manifestations of chauvinism, he has publicly come out against excessive flag-waving and band-playing.

"Dignity does not need pomposity to uphold it," he has said, "and pomposity in all its forms is a wrong."

Nyerere is a Catholic, with eight children, and his no less pronounced religious bent—Africa's first Cardinal lives in Dar es Salaam—sometimes confounds distant critics who consider him an unregenerate left-winger. "How can people say we're Communists of any kind," Lady Chesham asked me, "when the President and I are both *practicing* Catholics? We are in fact disliked just as much by the Eastern bloc of nations as by the West, because if we make a success of our *ujamaa* brand of socialism it will suggest that the Eastern countries had an erroneous approach to socialism. If *ujamaa* were genuinely Communistic, we'd have been able to move much more quickly toward achieving our goals."

Nyerere was educated, in the old-fashioned, imperialistic fashion, at the University of Edinburgh. In language, in law, in libertarian philosophy, he still feels an affinity to the British, and while he has lately been sympathetic to Russians and Chinese with ideological outlooks remote from those of his bygone mentors, it makes him unhappy when his newer friends too vehemently attack his older ones. Thus, when Stokely Carmichael, a couple of years ago, was, like other radical expatriates, contemplating permanent residence in Tanzania, and he made a fiery, anti-imperialist speech in Dar, Nyerere said that he'd have to simmer down or move along. So Carmichael packed up and went to Guinea, where no holds are barred. Nonetheless, there is probably more political militancy in Tanzania than anywhere else in East Africa; a couple of Nyerere's cabinet ministers seem to find it distressing, if not acutely painful, to engage in official diplomatic intercourse with the United States. Nations of all ideological stripes are represented in Dar es Salaam, and Nyerere's government has passed a law saying, in effect, that no foreign government in Tanzania may distribute material attacking any other foreign government with which the country has good relations. The North Koreans in Dar, and, to a lesser extent, the Chinese, have ignored this pronouncement, but there is no evidence that they have been reprimanded for breaking the local ground rules.

President Nyerere has gone to considerable lengths to ensure that the high officials of his government embrace probity of be-

173

havior. He keeps an observant eye on neighboring Kenya, some of whose high officials, as a result of acquiring choice tracts of land in a once white residential area, have become known, with more contempt than affection, as the "Banana Hills boys." Nyerere's espousal of honesty has had a discernible impact on his associates: Tanzania is one of the few African countries in which a substantial portion—sometimes as much as fifty percent—of all foreign-aid money and goods does not vanish before it reaches its intended recipients. Nyerere resides not in a fancy presidential palace, though he has one for state occasions, but in a house that he built himself and on which he is still paying off the mortgage. A few years ago, sizing up his countrymen and concluding that they were becoming too materialistic, the Mwalimo astonished them by imposing a thirty-percent pay cut on himself, making his cabinet ministers follow suit, and forbidding them to augment their incomes through nongovernmental activities. His salary is now only eighty-five hundred dollars a year.

It has been easier for Nyerere to assume a high moral stance than it might be for some of his contemporary leaders in Africa; he does not always have to weigh the tribal consequences of his actions. Tanzania has its hundred and twenty tribes—one for every hundred thousand people—but none of them are *political* entities. And Nyerere, coming from one of the smallest, could hardly be accused of trying to establish a tribal dynasty. He has been further fortunate in that Tanzania does not have a multiplicity of competing native languages, and has readily accepted Swahili as a universal national tongue. Since 1967, the official proceedings of Parliament have been printed in Swahili (though members may use English also if they like). The University of Dar es Salaam has an institute wholly devoted to research in Swahili, and Dar's Hotel Kilimanjaro is singular among East African hostels in that its public signs are rendered in both Swahili and English—"*Malipo*-Cashier," "*Simu*-Phones," "*Maelezo*-Information," and so on. The head of Tanzania's leading publishing house has translated Mao's *Guerrilla Tactics* into Swahili, and Shakespeare's *Merchant of Venice* and *Julius Caesar* were given the same honored treatment by no other than Julius Nyerere himself. When the British Broadcasting Corporation put on a radio version of the president's translation of *The Merchant of Venice*, it was rumored in Dar es Salaam that he had broken his own rule about accepting outside income; his publisher quickly announced that his proceeds from the broadcast, which totaled less than twenty-five dollars, would, like the more substantial royalties from his many books, be distributed to Tanzanian charities.

Swahili, a language that is about five-sixths Bantu and one-sixth Arabic, originated on Zanzibar. It is one of that island's few stabilizing contributions, so far, to the nation of which, since 1964, it has been a nomenclatural part. The first vice-president of Tanzania is also the chief of the Revolutionary Council of Zanzibar, which is a very independent part of Tanzania. Notwithstanding President Nyerere's strongly expressed disapproval of excesses in patriotism, on Zanzibar everybody is supposed to stop doing whatever he's doing and salute when the flag is raised in the morning and lowered in the evening.

Zanzibar is independently wealthy. It used to be a flourishing slave station; now it prospers from cloves, which are a major ingredient of, among other things, the aromatic cigarettes that are smoked by the billions in Indonesia. Zanzibar likes to flaunt its riches. When the mainland government pledged nine thousand dollars in emergency-relief funds to Pakistan after the 1970 tidal wave there, Zanzibar topped that with a fifty-four-thousand-dollar pledge all on its own. Zanzibar has outdone most African areas, including the Tanzanian mainland, in according hospitality to the People's Republic of China. Only about four hundred Chinese live on the island, but they are influential. There are a number of Chinese doctors on the staff of its hospital, which is named after Lenin. Peking gave Zanzibar an eight-hundred-and-seventy-thousand-dollar soccer stadium; and the principal orator at the island's recent observance of the anniversary of its independence day was the resident Chinese consul.

16

The activities of the Communist Chinese on the Tanzanian mainland have, in the last few years, caused much concern among outsiders who like to judge countries by the company they regularly keep. Tanzania's twelve-thousand-man army is largely Chinese-trained and -equipped. Quite a few Tanzanians have been to China, though perhaps not as many as the Chinese would have wished; Africans find it difficult to adjust to the puritanical Chinese attitudes toward sex and drinking. The Chinese have gone to extraordinary lengths to be nice to those Tanzanians, mostly members of trade missions, who have ventured their way; in Peking, one Tanzanian left a used razor blade in his hotel bathroom, and six weeks later the blade was politely returned to him by the Chinese Embassy in Dar es Salaam. The Chinese assign top-drawer diplomats to Tanzania, who behave with exemplary punctiliousness.

There is not a single American journalist permanently based in Dar; there are three Chinese correspondents. What brought them to the scene was, principally, the much-discussed railroad that the Chinese began building, in the fall of 1970, to link Dar es Salaam with Lusaka, eleven hundred and sixteen miles to the southwest in

Zambia. Scheduled to be finished before the end of 1975, and known as the Tan-Zam Railway, its cost—to be borne equally by Tanzania and Zambia—is expected to be slightly more than four hundred million dollars. The two countries started visualizing such a rail connection soon after they became independent, and for several years they tried to swing a loan to pay it. Tanzania and Zambia are sometimes chided by the West for getting themselves heavily involved with the Chinese, but the fact was that before approaching Peking, the two nations had appealed to, and been turned down by, the United States, Great Britain, West Germany, the Soviet Union, and the World Bank. The United States begged off partly because it already had a thirty-million-dollar commitment to cover about half the cost of a two-lane highway that was planned (and is now under construction also) along a route roughly parallel to that of the railroad; and partly because the rail line just didn't seem feasible—having stronger political than economic justification.

"You Americans kept telling us that the railroad would be a luxury," a Zambian minister told me. "Well, we are not persuaded that our heavy rains won't wash out the best of tarmac roads. What chiefly disturbs us Africans, though, is that the Western powers are always eager to tell us what we want, or what they think we want. The Eastern powers, instead, listen to our requests and then tell us how we can achieve them within the context of our needs. Moreover, it was not Mao Tse-tung who first dreamt of this kind of railroad, nor even Julius Nyerere or Kenneth Kaunda. It was Cecil Rhodes, and he wanted it to run not just from Dar to Lusaka but all the way from Cairo to Cape Town."

The Chinese listened, and then they came through with an exceedingly attractive proposition: an interest-free loan to cover the cost of construction, with repayment of the principal to be spread over thirty years, and no installments to be paid at all before 1983. Moreover, they would supervise the project themselves. As a result, there are more than ten thousand Chinese today in Tanzania, at which end of the line construction began. They live very unobtrusively—there is only one Chinese restaurant in Dar —which pleases Nyerere; their frugality is in the best *ujamaa* tradition. They have built their own residential enclaves, complete with rice paddies. Most of the Chinese are soldiers in mufti, but that is not particularly significant; the railroads within China, too, are constructed by the People's Liberation Army. One of their supply bases that I visited in Dar es Salaam looked like an American depot in Vietnam: there were brand-new, heavy-equipment vehicles lined up by the dozens—trucks, bulldozers, cranes, and concrete mixers—as well as bridge sections, lengths of track, engines, freight cars, and cabooses. Every signal box, every cross-tie, every length of wire for the project was being shipped from China. So many Chinese vessels were steaming in and out of Dar's narrow harbor that American companies had raised their freight rates, arguing that they were being subjected to intolerable delays because the Chinese were monopolizing the berths at the municipal piers. The Chinese contingent had only a few women in its ranks, principally nurses at a hospital the visitors also built for themselves, and since the men were hardly ever seen downtown, it was suspected by some onlookers that the ships must also be bringing in large doses of saltpeter.

Naturally, the presence of so many mainland Chinese in one spot outside of China became a magnet, especially in the pre-Ping-Pong days, for Western Sinologists. The United States has a limited number of senior foreign-service officers who are fluent in Chinese and knowledgeable about China; one of these experts, as the Tan-Zam railway got under way, was posted to the American Embassy at Dar es Salaam. His contacts with Chinese were courteous but cool. There was closer, and more choleric, contact one day in 1970 at a river bank in rural Tanzania, where an American construction crew working on a bridge site for the highway got into a hassle over rights of way with a Chinese construction crew working on a bridge site for the railroad. At one point, the Chinese held a handful of Americans captive there for several hours, and before the Tanzanian government interceded and got them released there was some pushing and shoving and scuffling and a few bruises—all things considered, probably as physical a confrontation as any Americans and Chinese had had since the Korean war.

The Chinese have promised that their railroad workers will leave when the job is finished, and Nyerere believes them. What benefits will Peking reap from tying up all that money and all those men for all those years? Well, for one thing, they will have demonstrated, on a scale as yet unduplicated anywhere, their capacity for creating a complex technological undertaking abroad. (And how especially triumphant for them, to be building, under close Western scrutiny, the kind of undertaking for which they are historically associated overseas with the ignominy of coolie labor!) For another, assuming that by 1975 Peking and Moscow are still at odds, a gaudy unveiling of a Tan-Zam Railway could surely be expected to put the Russians' noses out of joint. Finally, perhaps most importantly, the Chinese hope to be remembered as the people who, when Africa's traditional friends spurned its entreaties, lent a helping hand, not to mention four hundred million-plus dollars. They may even, despite their protestations of no long-term ambitions, be looking for a future base of operations, or at least an observation post, from which they can watch Southern Africa and the Indian Ocean. "Nyerere is no fool," I was told by an Englishman in Dar es Salaam who was anything but a fool himself. "He says if there's any sign of the Chinese getting out of control around here, he'll curb them. But will he? Can he ride the tiger? Or will it swallow him?"

The completion of the railroad should be especially gratifying to Zambia, because it will diminish that country's galling economic dependence—all the more upsetting considering that Zambia, like Tanzania, has embarked on a socialistic path—on the unabashedly nonsocialistic areas that abut it: Rhodesia and South Africa to its south, Mozambique to its east, and Angola to its west. (Rhodesia, once it embarked on its stubborn, anti-British path, enjoyed no formal diplomatic relations with the United States; American foreign service officers in that part of the world would sometimes demonstrate their derring-do by going to Victoria Falls, at the Zambian-Rhodesian border, and taking one bold step across a white stripe painted on a bridge there to designate the boundary line. If anybody caught them, they could always say they were pushed.)

Zambia—Northern Rhodesia in its colonial incarnation—has had an ambivalent relationship with its neighbors. President Kaunda has referred to his country as "Britain's sacrificial lamb on

the altar of Central Africa's settlers' whims." The expatriate settlers there came mostly from the south; many had Boer names
and the harsh racial attitudes that went with them. Northern
Rhodesia was only a protectorate, and it never had a good colonial
administration. Zambians today, accordingly, are on the whole
more suspicious of white foreigners than are other black East
Africans. Kaunda is constantly preaching the theoretical virtues
of a multiracial society; he has to, to neutralize automatic inbred
resistance to the notion. Zambia is a copper country—the third
largest producer on earth, after the United States and the Soviet
Union—and the mining money always used to end up down in
Salisbury, in southern Rhodesia, where the mining officials se-
questered themselves.

Since Zambia became independent, in 1964, after the breakup
of the experimental Federation of Rhodesia and Nyasaland (now
Malawi), it has been trying to shake loose from its long-standing
Rhodesian leash. In the five years from 1965 to 1970, Zambia
managed to reduce its imports from Rhodesia from about eighty
million dollars to three million. In 1966, Zambia began mining
its own coal, so it wouldn't have to look to Rhodesia for that re-
source. The following year, it put through a pipeline to Tanzania,
which eliminated its dependence on Rhodesian oil. While the
line was being constructed, Zambians were on strict gas rationing,
and even cabinet ministers went to their offices by bicycle, an
unusually humble means of transportation for Africans of that
stature. Zambia has not yet weaned itself from reliance on electricity generated in Rhodesia.

Zambia does not have radio-transmitting facilities powerful
enough to reach the white-dominated areas to its south. Radio
South Africa, on the other hand, regularly beams programs in its
direction, and Zambians are resigned to hearing, loud and clear,
all sorts of lurid and unflattering tales about themselves and their
black allies. It delights them when they can get a measure of re-
venge. One can only imagine with what glee the editors of the
daily *Times of Zambia* came upon, and duly featured, a dispatch
from Salisbury telling of a white tavern proprietor there who was
alleged to be farming out amenable women, including his own
wife, to liven things up at "Rent-a-Drunk" parties. But it is char-

acteristic of the complex economic realities of Africa that the *Times of Zambia* itself belongs to an international corporation called Lonrho (London-Rhodesia), which, with airy disregard for political differences, is active in Ghana and Nigeria, as well as in Lesotho and South Africa.

It is sometimes said in Africa that whatever Nyerere did yesterday, Kaunda will do tomorrow. The two presidents telephone each other every so often to arrange an informal get-together at their common border. As Nyerere demanded that his cabinet ministers eschew material rewards, so did Kaunda issue a leadership code. He even decreed, in November, 1970, that each of his ministers must personally cultivate at least two rural acres. Not long after Tanzania nationalized most of its industries, Zambia followed suit, much of the expropriation taking place on April 19, 1968, which has been known ever since as Fifty-one Per Cent Day. And Zambia has its own *ujamaa*-like resettlement program.

President Kaunda, who is known to his citizenry as "K. K.," is very strong on agriculture. He decreed 1971 "the year of the peasant," in the hope of thereby somehow increasing production of crops; one of Zambia's longstanding problems has been that, for Africa, it is highly urbanized, and has always had to import considerable quantities of food. But the funds Zambia had had to allocate for that had until recently been easy enough to come by, because of all the money that mining was bringing in. Copper accounts for ninety percent of the nation's exports, and more than half of its gross national product. Of Zambia's four and a half million people, more than eight hundred thousand live in the north central area where the mines are located, and into which the tip of the Katanga province of the Congo, a pedicle itself rich in ore, daintily thrusts. In Zambia's cabinet there is a Copper Belt Minister, and among its television viewers "The Flying Nun" must compete for ratings with "Around the Copper Belt." In 1970, however, the price of copper dropped, and on top of that came a disastrous cave-in at one of the big mines, resulting in a loss of seventy million dollars in income from that single lode.

The copper mines have been duly nationalized. It was easy enough for Zambia to take over its standard fifty-one percent of the companies, but reshuffling their staffs was something else again. The mining industry employs two thousand engineers; only five are Zambians, and it will be quite some time before many others can be trained to join them. Of the forty-three thousand employees of the mining companies, forty-five hundred—most of these in white-collar jobs—are expatriates. They come principally from South Africa and Rhodesia, their children attend schools in Salisbury, and they travel frequently to the white-dominated south. It is typical of the Zambian dilemma that while for political reasons the country forbids scheduled air service from Lusaka to South Africa, for practical reasons it condones it. Botswana Airways has three flights a week that theoretically terminate at Gaborone, in Botswana; but when they get there the same planes take the same passengers on to Johannesburg, after changing their flight numbers for appearance's sake.

However much Zambia would like to terminate all its trade with the south, it cannot do so because it has no other easy way of providing the amenities without which the expatriates on whom it depends might decide to leave. When the importation of consumer goods from South Africa was shut off for a while and these had to be trucked in from Dar es Salaam, the price of Corn Flakes went up by fifty percent. So there has developed an unwritten understanding that Zambia will export some of its copper through Rhodesia, which needs the money it gets from transshipment charges, and that in turn South Africa will keep at a reasonable level the price of its exports to Zambia—along with food products and explosives and machine parts that are needed for the mines.

Zambia's reluctant dependence on countries it despises is a constant source of friction. While I was in Lusaka, a government official told me that Zambia had just recently had to throw away fifty tons of onions that had been ordered from South Africa but that Rhodesia had delayed so long in transit, out of some momentary petulance, that the consignment had rotted. Not long afterward, Zambia found itself short of bread, because the seaport of Beira, in Mozambique, wouldn't transship flour and sacks to Zambian mills dependent on them. President Kaunda tries gamely to keep his balance on the tight wire of his predicament. "There is a key factor in retaining expatriate skills, which are still crucial for the mines," he said several months ago, "and one which the politicians would do well to leave alone."

Kaunda, when not trying to cope with the practicalities of economic survival, is an ardent advocate of humanism. Passengers on Zambia Airways (which has no southbound flights) are likely to find in their seat pockets little tracts of his authorship entitled "10 Thoughts on Humanism." Lately, though, most of his thoughts have inevitably had to be concentrated on what he views as inhumanism—the treatment by white southern Africans of their black compatriots. "We are not interested in the quarrel between East and West," he told his parliament. "We are interested in our freedom, in our security, in the freedom of our brothers in the south." Presumably to enhance that security, in April, 1968, Kaunda began an exchange of private letters with Prime Minister Vorster, although the Zambian leader's public stance had always been resolutely against any dialogue with the South African until his country mended its ways and aligned itself with the Lusaka Manifesto proclaimed by an OAU summit conference in 1969, according to the terms of which black Africa would restrain the military activities of its liberation groups if South Africa would embark on a program of "peaceful progress to emancipation" of its own downtrodden blacks. Early in 1971, Vorster made his correspondence with Kaunda public. There were no substantive revelations; indeed, the correspondence indicated that Kaunda had rejected Vorster's suggestion that the two men meet. Apparently, the South African divulged the exchange of letters chiefly to embarrass the Zambian, who was the incumbent chairman of the OAU, which had never exchanged anything with South Africa except invective.

The OAU has a Liberation Committee, which is supposed to help the freedom fighters who hope by force to depose the white minority rulers of South Africa, Rhodesia, Mozambique, and Angola. But most of the actual help these relatively small bands of idealists and optimists have got has come not from their fellow Africans but from Russia and China. Nyerere and Kaunda have been their chief African benefactors. Kaunda, aware that his national armed forces consist of just two battalions, which South

Africa, if it chose, could wipe out overnight, has to be prudent in his support of the liberation-front movements. He has forbidden them to engage in military training or to traffic in arms within Zambia's boundaries. At the same time, since 1966 he has provided rent-free headquarters for them in Lusaka at a curious installation called the Liberation Center. Its very name has a brave ring, and its entrance is surmounted by the clarion cry "Victory or death."

The Center, a cluster of one-story brick cubicles built around a grassy courtyard, houses the representatives—each with his revolutionary organization's name neatly posted above his door—of the African National Congress (which aims to liberate South Africa), FRELIMO (Mozambique), ZAPU (Rhodesia), SWAPO (South West Africa), and MPLA (Angola). The men sitting behind the desks inside look like aging, tired, underpaid bureaucrats, which is what in the main they are. Still, it is touching to meet them— Africans who have been struggling against the white governments of their homelands (from which they are permanently barred) for twenty, thirty, or forty years, and who cite their long case histories of harassment and imprisonment like soldiers rattling off their combat experiences. They all talk freely enough to visitors— one gets the impression that they are eager to have somebody to talk *to*—but when they are asked about the numbers of freedom fighters or details of clandestine operations, they are understandably uncommunicative. A spokesman for the ANC told me with grudging admiration for his particular enemy that while his group had managed recently to intensify its exhortatory broadcasts to South Africa, the government there had countered by mass-producing cheap radios for sale to blacks—radios ingeniously designed to receive merely programs of lulling music produced within South Africa.

The FRELIMO office seemed the busiest, as well it might have, for that group and its anti-Portuguese allies have kept one hundred and twenty-five thousand Portuguese soldiers tied down in Portugal's African colonies, a huge drain on the resources and manpower of the European country. The FRELIMO agent at the Center said that it might take another fifty years to drive the Portuguese out of Africa, but that his people were not discouraged; they had

185

learned long ago to be patient. They had been *encouraged*, he went on, cheerfully, by a conference of liberation groups in Italy some months previous—gratified, for one thing, that a NATO country had permitted them to meet, and, for another, that the Pope had granted some of them an audience. "The Catholic church in Mozambique sides with the Portuguese, inevitably," the FRELIMO man said, "but the Pope's reception surely indicated that he didn't think we were terrorists or Communists. If we'd been Communists, we wouldn't have asked to see him, and if we were terrorists, he wouldn't have seen us."

Now, he went on, they were girding themselves for an all-out assault on a new looming objective, the Cabora Bossa Dam, a project that has been cited by many black Africans as a classic example of how little the rest of the world cares about their feelings. The dam, a five-hundred-million-dollar undertaking in Mozambique on the Zambesi River, eighty miles from the Zambian border, is being financed by companies from half a dozen countries, including England and West Germany, and it is expected to provide fifty billion kilowatts of power annually to South Africa, Rhodesia, and Mozambique. American, Swedish, and Italian groups were in the consortium initially, but pulled out, largely for political reasons. (The General Electric Company backed off, for instance, when the United States government wouldn't endorse its application to the World Bank for a fifty-five-million-dollar loan to underwrite its participation.) Willy Brandt was asked while on his East African holiday if Germany might not quit, too, but he had replied that to change plans would create an atmosphere of insecurity in Africa. But the specter of the dam itself, destined to make the already powerful even more potent, was creating precisely that insecurity in independent black Africa. The FRELIMO man, now no longer cheerful but scowling, told me that while fighting the Portuguese in Mozambique his soldiers were careful to spare civilians, but that the dam had been classified a military objective, and any civilians who worked on it or even lived in the vicinity of it would be considered fair game. Such threats had, of course, already come to the attention of the alert intelligence services of the southern African states, and the top security officers of South Africa, Rhodesia, Angola, and Mozambique were right then meeting in Salisbury to discuss FRELIMO and its intentions toward the Cabora Bossa project. Perhaps before the dam produces any electricity the dialogue that Houphouët-Boigny and a few other black leaders hope to initiate with South Africa will have taken place, and there will be some easing of the long-standing tensions between the irreconcilables of the continent. Meanwhile, at the Liberation Center in Lusaka, the black exiles from white-run southern Africa will continue to churn out their angry tracts, stoically awaiting the day when all Africans will have a chance to share, in their own homelands, the joys and perils and frustrations of the freedom—even if only that relative freedom that a military government allows—that now exists, both tenuously and tenaciously, in independent black Africa.

INDEX

INDEX

INDEX

Lee, Robert E., 80
Liberia, 29, 67–75
    black Jews in, 76
    borders of, 55–56
    citizenship in, 73
    customs of, 69–70, 73–74
    economy of, 43, 71
    education in, 102
    Israel and, 113
    literacy in, 32
    stability of, 29
    Tubman and, 23–25, 70–71
    United States and, 67–69, 71, 73–75
Literacy, 32–33
Livingston, David, 168
Lo Liyong, Taban, 9–11, 21
Lumumba University, 100
Luos, 154

Masai, 158–59
Mayer, Moshe, 61–62
Mazrui, Ali, 21, 24, 43
Mboya, Tom, 154
Migration, 46–47
Missionaries, 105–7
Mobutu, Joseph, 26, 110–12, 116, 119
Moi, Daniel arap, 153
Mozambique, 184–87
Mulele, Pierre, 109
Munro, Eleanor, 11
Mutesa, Sir Edward, II, 139

Nasser, Gamal, 120
National Broadcasting Company, 73–74
Nationalism, 43–45
Natural resources, distribution of, 42–43
Newsom, David, 72
Newspapers, 33–35
Niger, 29
Nigeria, 71, 119–34
    agriculture in, 131–32
    army of, 120
    Biafra and, 121–29
    Britain and, 48
    crime in, 133–34
    education in, 97, 99, 101, 105
    importance of, 18
    James Brown in, 78
    literacy rate in, 32
    newspapers in, 34–35
    oil in, 129–31
    population of, 30
    provinces of, 119–20
    stability of, 29
    transportation in, 132–33
    tribes in, 44, 119–21
    Zaire compared to, 119
Nixon, Richard, 25
Nkrumah, Kwame, 10, 20–24, 44, 136, 141, 145
Nsukka University, 99
Nyerere, Julius, 26, 96, 105, 139–41, 149–50, 170–75, 178–80, 182, 184

Obote, Apolo Milton, 72, 137–45, 150
Odhiambo, Thomas, 158

Odinga, Oginga, 154
Oil, 129–31
Ojukwu, Sir Louis, 125
Ojukwu, Odumegwu, 24, 121, 123

Passman, Otto E., 71
Paul VI, Pope, 143–44
Pirbhai, Sir Eboo, 164
Pompidou, Georges, 48
Population, growth of, 30–32
Portugal, 129, 185–86
Powell, Enoch, 165

Rassemblement Démocratique Africain, 59
Regional organizations, 41–43
Religion, 105–9
Rhodes, Cecil, 178
Rhodesia, 180–81, 184–86
Rockefeller Foundation, 131
Roosevelt, Franklin D., Jr., 74
Rwanda, 29

San Juan, Puerto Rico, 87
Sedar-Senghor, Leopold, 32, 49
Senegal
    China and, 116
    economy of, 43, 56–57
    education in, 98, 103–4
    The Gambia and, 56
    Israel and, 113
    literacy rate in, 32
    stability of, 29, 57–58
Sierra Leone, 29, 43
Simpson, Billy, 74
Sivomey, Marie, 86–87
Slavery, 79–81
Smuggling, 47
Socialism in Uganda, 139–40
Somalia, 151
South Africa, Republic of, 186
    British arms sales to, 140–41
    Houphouët-Boigny and, 63–65, 187
    Israel and, 113
    Kaunda and, 184–85
South-West Africa, 185
Stanley, Henry, 168
Students, 100–4; see also Education
Sudan, 149

Tanzania, 169–80
    Asians in, 166–68
    Britain and, 48
    China and, 152, 177–80
    coup in, 136
    in East African Community, 149–53, 156
    education in, 96–99
    Israel and, 113
    James Brown in, 79
    Nyerere and, 172–75
    stability of, 29
    tourism in, 156–57
    tribes in, 174
    Ujamaa program in, 170–73
    white people in, 18–19, 169–70
Taiwan, 115–17

191

INDEX